Thank You for Your Leadership

The Power of Distributed Leadership in a Digital Conversion Model

MARK A. EDWARDS

*Superintendent,
Mooresville Graded School District,
North Carolina*

PEARSON

Boston • Columbus • Indianapolis • New York • San Francisco • Hoboken
Amsterdam • Cape Town • Dubai • London • Madrid • Milan • Munich • Paris • Montreal • Toronto
Delhi • Mexico City • São Paulo • Sydney • Hong Kong • Seoul • Singapore • Taipei • Tokyo

Vice President & Editorial Director: Jeffrey W. Johnston
Executive Editor: Meredith D. Fossel
Program Manager: Maren L. Beckman
Editorial Assistant: Maria Feliberty
Development Editors: Diane Rapley, Linda Bishop
Director of Marketing: Margaret Waples
Marketing Manager: Christopher Barry
Project Management Team Lead: JoEllen Gohr
Project Manager: Jessica H. Sykes
Procurement Specialist: Deidra Skahill
Senior Art Director: Diane Lorenzo
Cover Designer: Diane Lorenzo
Full-Service Project Management: Cenveo® Publisher Services
Composition: Cenveo® Publisher Services
Printer/Binder: LSC Communications
Cover Printer: LSC Communications
Text Font: Minion Pro

Library of Congress Cataloging in Publication Control Number: 2014044321

8 17

PEARSON

ISBN-10: 0-13-356318-9
ISBN-13: 978-0-13-356318-4

About the Author

Dr. Mark Edwards has served as a public school superintendent for over twenty years, in Henrico County and Danville, Virginia, and since 2007 in the Mooresville Graded School District in North Carolina, where he has led a widely recognized digital conversion initiative.

Dr. Edwards graduated from the University of Tennessee and received his doctoral degree from Vanderbilt University. He has served as a teacher, coach, principal, and college dean and as the vice president of Harcourt Assessment. He comes from a family of educators and is a tireless advocate for public education.

Dr. Edwards was named Virginia Superintendent of the Year in 2001, North Carolina Superintendent of the Year in 2012, and AASA National Superintendent of the Year in 2013. He has also been recognized as the 1998 Virginia Superintendent of the Year by the Virginia Library Association, the 2000 Virginia Superintendent of the Year by the Virginia Music Association, and the 2014 North Carolina Superintendent of the Year by the North Carolina Art Association. Other awards include the 2003 Harold McGraw Prize in Education, the 2014 North Carolina Forum Jay Robinson Leadership award, and the 2014 North Carolina Order of the Long Leaf Pine.

Dr. Edwards currently serves as the chairman of the League of Innovative Schools advisory board and as president of the North Carolina Superintendents' Association. He is considered an expert on North Carolina antique art pottery, loves cheering on his son Luke's sports teams, and is an enthusiastic fan of music of all kinds.

Acknowledgments

Thank you MGSD students for your leadership, enthusiasm, exuberance, and love of learning. Thank you MGSD teachers, administrators, staff, parents, school board, community members, and elected officials for modeling leadership with your relentless belief in every child, every day.

Thank you to the fantastic editorial team of Diane Rapley, Linda Bishop, and Tanae McLean. Special thanks to Pearson leaders Meredith Fossel and Steve Gross for your support, encouragement, and belief in this work. Thank you Michael Fullan for your leadership!

Thank you to superintendent colleagues Matt Aiken, Rosa Atkins, Russell Booker, Bruce Borchers, Bobby Browder, Linda Clark, Dallas Dance, Dan Domenech, Chuck Fowler, Pat Greco, Terry Grier, John Harper, Bill Hite, Steve Joel, Eric Jones, Chris Johns, Pat Kinlaw, Damian La Croix, Lorraine Lange, Lynn Moody, Heath Morrison, Steve Murley, David Myers, Katrise Perera, James Ponce, David Shuler, Kevin Singer, Aaron Spence, Tom Trigg, Steve Webb, Mike Winstead, and Donna Wright for your leadership and conviction for children.

Thanks to Crystal, Ingrid, Scott, Stephen, Terry, and Todd for your constant lift.

Thanks to Marcia, Adrian, Autumn, and Luke for your inspiration. Thanks to my all-time favorite teachers Bill and Erne Edwards.

And thanks to every public school teacher in the United States and across the globe for building our future!

Contents

Foreword

One of the most difficult things to address in schools these days is the development of a shared vision. Visions on paper abound, but the key is to make the ideas shared and grounded. There is only one way to accomplish this, and that is to have leaders at all levels working, interacting, examining impact, and learning from implementation.

This work must be transparent and widespread with people seeing what works and articulating to each other and to external visitors exactly what they are doing and with what results, constantly aligning the vision with leadership for action. Under these circumstances it is possible to be focused and adaptable while processing all kinds of feedback from internal and external sources.

Thank You for Your Leadership describes how ubiquitous, shared leadership has allowed the Mooresville Graded School District (MGSD) to successfully integrate its vision throughout the culture. What is most impressive about the MGSD culture is that leadership is locked in every nook and cranny of the district. It is impossible to be a member of the system without finding oneself drawn into leadership. Every chapter of this book outlines examples of leadership on the part of MGSD district members.

The book shows that a radically new view of leadership is required for sustainability, what the author calls "second-order leadership," that integrates leadership into every aspect of district life, from hiring procedures to student and parent leadership. From the day teachers are hired into MGSD, they are pre-selected and cultivated for leadership, not only as individuals but also as members of multiple teams. They learn to lead through any number of roles, and in several formal and informal leadership programs.

This is not just a plan on paper. The book is full of statements by leaders within the district and by countless visitors showing that focused leadership is happening on the ground and permeating the system. These accounts are not only confirming, they also give the reader great, grounded ideas about what needs to be done and how to do it.

In my work I have identified three powerful forces for deep learning—pedagogy; change knowledge, especially change leadership; and technology. I have written that these three domains have grown over the years, but unfortunately independently of each other, and in order to make learning "irresistibly engaging," the three domains must be integrated to the point of synergy. Mark Edwards and his team at MGSD have done just that—combining powerful pedagogy and digital conversion driven and supported by widespread focused leadership throughout the system.

Thank You for Your Leadership does not avoid discussion of the "tough stuff" that all schools face. It shows how districts can be supportive, love their employees, eliminate silos, contribute to growth, still give hard feedback, and when necessary let people go. Since the overall stance is growth-oriented and the whole system is involved, the vast majority of people do develop, leaving just a few who must be dealt with along the way. If the climate is positive and developmental, when problems arise, it is likely that peers will accept and even welcome actions that support overall success.

The intensive and comprehensive focus on teaching and learning at MGSD is characterized by pervasive digital resources for students and teachers alike, an interactive and highly focused student and staff culture, a personal quest for excellence that incorporates data and growth, an evolving systemic team, a shared emphasis on learning, and a constant focus on student achievement. The end result is that students at MGSD have achieved impressive new levels of academic achievement across all groups.

Thank You for Your Leadership shows how the MGSD digital conversion initiative, deeply integrated with pedagogy, is the work of interlocking leaders throughout the system, a culture of learning brought to life by leaders who share the same vision and methodology. Most of the advances in learning linked to digital devices are found in individual schools, and it is very rare to find digitally immersed learning in a whole district. This is what makes *Thank You for Your Leadership* a unique book.

Readers will learn what is possible today and what the future offers. MGSD, more than any other district, is in a position to lead the charge into the next generation of school districts that go deep into the culture of digitally based learning and leadership.

—Michael Fullan,
author and former dean,
Ontario Institute for Studies in Education

Prologue

Moving Toward a New View of Leadership

"The force of leadership distributed across many team members has a powerful impact on student achievement."

One day in June 2012, as I hurried toward the TSA screening area on my way to Washington, D.C., I saw that the line was long, and I started worrying about missing my flight. I could see the usual assortment of business passengers on their cell phones, a couple of families headed toward vacation, and a few other people I could not classify as easily. Most passengers seemed a little impatient or apprehensive, as they usually do, but I looked to the front of the line and noticed that the atmosphere up front was unusually jovial. I was intrigued.

As I got closer to the checkpoint, I started to understand what was going on. I heard the TSA attendant ask with a huge grin, "Mr. Nelson, how are you doing today?" "I'm doing okay," the passenger smiled back. "Well, I hope you have a great day," she responded pleasantly. When the next passenger arrived at her checkpoint, she said, "Don't you look nice today, Ms. Weiss." "Well, you just made my day," the lady responded. "Travel safe," the attendant offered with another smile.

This continued with every person in line. Everyone was affected by the attendant's cheerfulness, kindness, and personal acknowledgement. When I handed her my driver's license, I was already smiling after observing the exchanges for five minutes. "Mr. Edwards, I hope you have a great trip," she said as she looked me in the eye. "Thank you," I replied. "You need to lead training sessions for all the TSA staff."

As I walked toward my gate, I thought about the impact of this one person on an environment that is often tense and aggravating. Because she was conducting mundane business with a personal touch and a smile, she was easily the best TSA person I had ever encountered. She was positively influencing passengers and modeling how to do the job for colleagues, all on her own initiative.

Although I doubt that she would match the generally accepted definition of a leader because she did not rank highly in the organization, to me she was clearly demonstrating leadership in action.

Learning about Leadership

My parents, both excellent career educators, immersed my siblings and me in a mixture of love, work ethic, and humor that has been part of my leadership makeup ever since. Based on a deep sense of honor for older, younger, and newer family members that shaped our daily lives, a connected family dynamic and cultural condition helped define us. From childhood on, educators and family members helped me learn to lead, so I have long viewed leadership opportunities as a natural part of my culture and a core personal value.

My formal leadership training began in 1988, when I was a graduate student at Vanderbilt University. I read Max De Pree's *Leadership Is an Art* and was impressed by his concepts of participatory leadership and culture as the driving force in organizations. I studied Roland Barth's work on learning, sharing, and collaborating as the foundations of school improvement. The work of Michael Fullan and Margaret Wheatley on organizational design made me an enthusiastic believer in the power of shared leadership and the science of organizational flow. Jonathan Kozol's emphasis on the moral imperative to serve our nation's most needy children and Malcom Gladwell's books on the psychology of societal evolution stirred my soul and further influenced my view of the responsibilities of leadership.

One of my first administrative assignments was as principal of Bay Haven Basics Plus Elementary School in Sarasota County, Florida, where I was fortunate to work with a superintendent, Chuck Fowler, who believed strongly in shared decision making and leading with courtesy and kindness, and who became—and still is—my mentor.

Later, when I was principal of Northfield Elementary in Murfreesboro, Tennessee, I worked with a great teacher, Jennifer Knox, who modeled the power of leadership at the teacher level. She was a constant "can do" force for the whole school, taking on more than her share of tough-to-teach kids because she was always able to reach them. One day, a social worker brought us a foster child who had been abused and passed around and who had serious behavior problems. Although Mrs. Knox already had a larger class than the other teachers, I knew she was the best person in the school to help the new little girl, Amy.

I talked it over with her and took Amy along to her classroom. When we arrived, Mrs. Knox said for all the students to hear, "Mr. Edwards, thank you so much! The girls were just saying that we have too many boys in this class, and we will love having you, Amy. Come on in here, and let's get you ready to go. Great news, class, this is Amy! Let's give her a big cheer!" I walked back down the hall knowing that Amy would thrive—and she did.

When I served as the superintendent in Henrico County, Virginia, our leadership team read Linda Lambert's *Building Leadership Capacity in Schools* and Margaret Wheatley's *Leadership and the New Science*, both of which profoundly impacted us personally and collectively. The ideas in those books drove us to accelerate our leadership capacity-building effort by designing ongoing leadership "pathways" for teachers.

Since 2007, I have been the superintendent of the Mooresville Graded School District (MGSD) in Mooresville, North Carolina, outside of Charlotte. As a principal, dean, and superintendent, I have observed leadership in schools, school systems, grade levels, departments, classrooms, communities, and organizations and consistently noted the impact of leaders on the culture of each group. My view of leadership has evolved and broadened beyond the general definition of school leadership, which focuses on strong individual leadership by principals and superintendents. Today, the evolving education ecosystem requires that school leaders grow their skills in the context of the needs of students and teachers and immerse themselves in the study and practice of distributed leadership as an art and science.

My many experiences with leaders at all levels have influenced me greatly, and I have used them to help build leaders during my career. I have learned over the years to encourage the unique talents of teachers and staff and move them toward leadership roles, to bring the maximum force to bear on improving student achievement.

Dr. Vicki Wilson, a colleague from the time I worked in Henrico County, said to me recently, "Mark, you've been implementing a different view of leadership for years, in all your different positions." It took me some time to consciously formulate my view of leadership, but I gradually began to realize that leadership like that shown by the TSA attendant—distributed throughout the organization and delivered at the point of service—is the most powerful and effective.

Today I consciously apply new leadership principles in my own work and try to foster them in others. I work with many teachers, principals, students, custodians, bus drivers, cafeteria workers, school board members, community members, and office staff who demonstrate leadership at their points of service, create positive experiences for others, and model the best way to do their jobs.

LEADERSHIP VOICE

Learning about Gratitude

By **Rebecca T. Miller**
Editor-in-Chief, School Library Journal

After the panel, . . . Edwards . . . greeted me by saying, "Thank you for your leadership." No one has ever said those particular words to me, and I would be surprised if many school librarians hear them often, if ever. The phrase articulated gratitude for past actions, and perhaps more importantly, expectation.

I thought about the gap between the many school librarians who are already leaders, and the administrators who may not know the potential role of these players in making better schools. This is the largest challenge facing this profession.

Effective Leadership Is Shared

At MGSD, hundreds of visitors come to study our digital conversion initiative every year, and their most frequent observation is not about our one-to-one technology or our digital tools but about our shared leadership, because we believe that leadership extends way beyond a few individuals. Today, leaders throughout MGSD influence our instructional practice and our school and district culture, to the benefit of every student.

Individuals and teams demonstrate frontline leadership by striving for greatness—taking the initiative to solve problems or improve processes. We encourage everyone to lead, and we recognize our leaders, subscribing to the belief that if we all lift, we will all be lifted.

VISITOR FEEDBACK   *"You seem to have leaders all over the place—teachers, principals, assistant principals, and other staff. So many leaders are creating a flow of energy—I can feel it."*

—Pat Greco
Superintendent, Menomonee Falls, Wisconsin

Our nation's schools are called on to address more complicated challenges than ever before and in circumstances where accountability is a must. One or two people at the top of an organization cannot successfully lead such an enormous effort. We must develop broad and deep leadership that is available to all in order to build the energy to drive us forward.

I believe that other schools and districts can replicate our collective leadership model with outstanding leaders who reach into classrooms, hallways, school buses, cafeterias, and every other corner of school life, no matter whether the task is to manage budgets, clean schools, feed students, build community, or improve student performance. With the enormous challenges of change

Chief technology officer Scott Smith working with Mooresville High School technology facilitator Tracey Waid on new online resources

management and digital conversion, multiple leaders are essential to this new way of life in our schools.

VISITOR FEEDBACK   *"Ask most district administrators today what their core mission is, and they likely will cite improving teaching and learning in schools. Teachers expect their superintendents to make decisions that support their work with students. Families expect their district leaders, along with principals and teachers, to provide their children with the highest quality education possible.*

"These expectations, combined with increasing accountability demands at the federal and state levels, have resulted in districts having to transition from being bureaucratic and compliance-focused to being mission-driven and results-focused.

"Adding to the challenge and complexity of this shift is the ever-changing impact that technology is having on how our students learn and, consequently, how we must teach and lead in response. Gone are the days of teachers being the sole source of knowledge for students to rely on. Now they are brokers of multiple sources of information, coaching and facilitating students as they learn how to be responsible, critical consumers of the information they find.

"Gone, too, are the days of leaders focusing merely on leading. Today's district leaders must focus on re-culturing their systems. Re-culturing goes far beyond altering structures and policies—or even reallocating resources. It demands that leaders clearly communicate a vision for what can be, along with tangible strategies that engage staff and, more importantly, help them experience that change is possible. It is only through changing people's experiences that we ultimately change their beliefs. Re-culturing, then, can occur only when the adults within a school district have a shared vision, strategy, and belief system for helping all students learn.

"Districts like Mooresville serve as models for what re-culturing can do—for both students and staff. Learning, teaching, and leading become more dynamic, collaborative, and personalized, with the emphasis being on asking the right questions rather than only knowing the right answers. This happens over time, however, and requires courage, self-reflection, tenacity, and an unrelenting belief in ourselves and our students."

—Dr. Susan Enfield
Superintendent, Highline School District, Burien, Washington

As I hurried down the hall at Park View Elementary, I turned the corner and saw a little boy in tears and a little girl comforting him. "What's the matter?" I asked them. "Jerry got lost on his way to the office," said the little girl. "But I told him I can show him the way, and it's going to be okay. I told him I got lost when I was in kindergarten, but now that I'm in first grade I know my way around, and I know where the office is. You don't have to keep walking with us." As I walked on to the meeting, I knew I had just seen the impact of leadership on both of these young learners.

REFERENCES

Barth, Roland S. (1990). *Improving Schools from Within: Teachers, Parents, and Principals Can Make the Difference.* San Francisco, CA: Jossey-Bass.

De Pree, Max. (1990). *Leadership Is an Art.* New York, NY: Dell.

Fullan, Michael. (2008). *The Six Secrets of Change: What the Best Leaders Do to Help Their Organizations Survive and Thrive.* San Francisco, CA: Jossey-Bass.

Gladwell, Malcolm. (2000). *The Tipping Point: How Little Things Can Make a Big Difference.* New York, NY: Little, Brown and Company.

Gladwell, Malcolm. (2008). *Outliers: The Story of Success.* New York, NY: Little, Brown and Company.

Kozol, Jonathan. (1991). *Savage Inequalities: Children in America's Schools.* New York, NY: Crown Publishing Group.

Lambert, Linda. (1998). *Building Leadership Capacity in Schools.* Alexandria, VA: Association for Supervision and Curriculum Development.

Miller, Rebecca T. (December 2013). "Take Your Place at the Table: Thrive as Part of the Solution Your School Needs." *School Library Journal.*

Wheatley, Margaret. (2006). *Leadership and the New Science: Discovering Order in a Chaotic World.* San Francisco, CA: Berrett-Koehler.

Chapter 1

Distributed Leadership and High-Performance Teaching and Learning

"High-performance teaching and learning are not possible with just one or two leaders at the top of an organization."

In the fall of 2012, Robin Melton, principal of East Mooresville Intermediate School, was walking out of the media center at her usual fast pace two days before school started, when she hit a slick spot on a newly waxed floor, fell, and fractured her vertebrae. Robin had done a tremendous job as principal, leading change, focusing on every student, and developing capacity and leadership in the faculty. The assistant principal, Jason Gardner, had been in his new role for only a few weeks.

The faculty and staff rose to the occasion, supporting Jason and the student body with collective leadership to fill in for Robin. The grade-level chairs stepped up their efforts to support their colleagues and each other. Jason immediately took a leadership role, and the staff was right there with him.

East Mooresville Intermediate School did not miss a beat in a situation that might have caused serious problems in many other schools. Everyone responded to the unexpected, nimbly and collectively. High-performance teaching and learning carried on without interruption, and the students recognized it.

In the Mooresville Graded School District (MGSD), we have many leaders—principals, teachers, custodians, central office staff, clerical workers, bus drivers, technology staff, child nutritionists, cafeteria workers, parents, students, and community members. This shared leadership brings a clarity and momentum to our work—what I call "high-performance teaching and learning."

We have leaders in every aspect of our daily work who influence everyone around them with their powerful enthusiasm and support. High-performance teaching and learning are not possible with just one or two leaders at the top of an organization. At MGSD, distributed leadership directly impacts student achievement every day.

What Is Distributed Leadership?

Distributed leadership in schools means that every employee, every community member, and every student has the opportunity to lead and is expected to lead—and that leadership is not solely reserved for those at the top.

In many organizations, leadership roles are set in stone, and others have little opportunity to lead. But we have found that if we reverse the mind-set and proactively encourage leadership—with both opportunities and expectations—many individuals and teams step up to the challenge. Distributed leadership moves beyond the traditional definition to a new way of thinking about how we lead in our schools.

The author and Mooresville High School 10th grader A'Lishia Bowman working with first graders at South Elementary School

Leaders at Every Level

Distributed leadership—also known as shared, collective, ubiquitous, or inclusive leadership—is found throughout our district because we have consciously built our culture on a distributed leadership model.

Teachers lead students with enthusiasm and love. Principals and other administrators lead in classrooms, hallways, and cafeterias, modeling attention to the work of the day. Student leaders help to establish a collective work ethic and a caring environment that sets the tone.

Custodians go the extra mile to influence the environment in which we work. Bus drivers know all the students and encourage them on a daily basis. Community members are active on many advisory boards. Community foundations support a variety of needs, and numerous community and civic organizations provide a collective lift that we feel and count on every day.

VISITOR FEEDBACK *"Great leaders understand the only way to embed change is by including others in the journey. Bringing change across a district is hard work. Internal momentum is obvious in MGSD, but so is momentum from working and sharing with districts from around the nation. The deep sense of team is making learning happen for students and staff."*

—Dr. Pat Greco
Superintendent of Menomonee Falls, Wisconsin,
and Member of the League of Innovative Schools

Roving Leaders

As described in *Every Child, Every Day*, teachers in MGSD operate as "roving conductors," moving around the classroom to orchestrate student work. Similarly, "roving leaders"—principals, assistant principals, central office leaders, teacher leaders, and others—orchestrate students and adults throughout our schools.

Roving leaders are there to step in whenever needed, help new staff members, and encourage students. They provide situational coaching and developmental direction for students and staff, who need encouragement from principals, assistant principals, and other leaders all the time.

Daily life in schools can be rife with distractions and conflict that make it difficult to sustain the rhythm of striving for excellence. To counteract these

Jason Gardner, principal of East Mooresville Middle School, visiting a sixth-grade class

forces, MGSD roving leaders stay visible, reinforce the culture of collective problem solving, and support the high-performance teaching and learning environment. If principals, superintendents, and other school leaders are highly visible and students see them in their classrooms and hallways every day, the messages are clear:

Roving Leader Messages

- This is where the action is.
- You—students and teachers—are my top priority.
- Stay focused.
- This is what matters.

The Impact of Distributed Leadership

In our schools today, we need to go beyond the traditional view of leadership, which assumes that large groups of people will follow the instructions of one or two people at the top and success will automatically follow. In fact, the opposite is generally true. At MGSD, we have adopted a culture of collective leadership because it leads to high-performance teaching and learning and greater student success.

Most schools and school systems try to build teamwork and collegiality. But I believe that MGSD's mission of sharing leadership responsibility has gone one step further and directly impacted student performance.

Peak-Performance Teaching and Learning

Good tennis players see the ball unusually clearly and hit almost every shot exactly where they want it to go. In team sports such as basketball, high-caliber athletes can reach amazing new levels of teamwork, functioning as one rather than as a group. Athletes achieve this "peak-performance zone" only after much practice and application. The same is true with teaching and learning.

When our constant efforts result in peak-performance teaching and learning, we have the feeling that everything is going right. At MGSD, many leaders work together to create high-performance zone conditions for individuals, groups, and teams, where the shared synergy enhances learning and workflow.

The efforts of employees "click" in a new way when people are influenced by the synergy of shared support and leadership. A new atmosphere develops, where everyone is called on to give his or her best because everyone is a leader. The feeling is contagious, and we are all able to take our game to new heights.

MGSD Four-Year Cohort Graduation Rate by Subgroup, 2005–2013

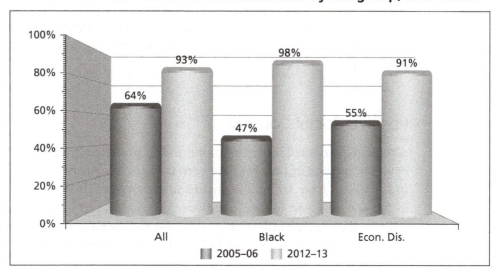

Because leaders are everywhere, the distributed leadership model influences every corner of school life. Everyone is inspired to join in and weave high-performance elements, such as the following, into every aspect of daily culture:

Elements of High-Performance Teaching and Learning

- Digital resources for research, projects, personal work, and collaboration
- An interactive, fluid, and highly focused student and staff culture
- A personal quest for excellence that incorporates data and offers nurturance to others
- An evolving systemic team
- A shared emphasis on learning
- A constant focus on student achievement

Increased Visibility

One or two leaders with limited visibility cannot create a high-performance teaching and learning zone. Traditional and hierarchical leaders are not only less visible to others, they are often unaware of what is going on in their schools because they are removed from much of the daily activity.

At MGSD, leaders are visible everywhere and engaged everywhere. They influence others while looking at school activity from different angles and bringing a variety of leadership perspectives to our collective work. They strive to be present as well as visible, in order to bring their leadership skills to bear on every situation they encounter.

Positive Social Context

Although distributed leadership is not widely practiced in schools, it is far from a new concept, and its benefits have been noted across many types of organizations. In *Leadership Is an Art*, businessman and author Max De Pree writes that in an inclusive work environment, employees feel needed, involved, and cared about as individuals. They are also treated fairly, able to take risks, believe that others try to understand their concerns, and feel that they are part of any success. When these attitudes and feelings are present, organizations flourish.

We have consciously nurtured these feelings at MGSD in order to create a positive social context in our classrooms and hallways that benefits employees and ultimately students.

Resilience and Perseverance

In MGSD's digital conversion initiative, distributed leadership has helped us build resilience and perseverance in spite of obstacles. Our journey toward personalized learning and digital tools has been full of challenges, but an abundance of leaders from throughout the community has allowed us to navigate the difficulties.

In our first years, many staff members had doubts, and some predicted failure, but more and more gradually caught the fever, supported by their colleagues. As a result, the resistance faded over time.

We prepared our staff for the turbulence that comes with change by telling people to hold together to ride it out. Maintaining focus throughout the change process was hard, and when turbulence hit, it was even harder. But when employees hit a bump in the road, they did not have to go up the chain of command to find a solution. They could be confident that a leader was nearby to help, and, as a result, they became more and more resilient when new problems came up.

Collectively, we were able to deal with the challenges promptly and move forward together, with renewed confidence in the effectiveness of our teamwork approach. Our distributed leadership model pushed leaders out into halls and classrooms to provide support and solve problems as needed.

VISITOR FEEDBACK   *"In MGSD, what you see are daily actions from all members of the community exhibiting critical leadership, which have resulted in increased student achievement through active student engagement. A positive school culture is the most powerful indicator of just how far school can go when everyone is considered, valued, and viewed as a leader!"*

—Dr. S. Dallas Dance
Superintendent, Baltimore County Schools, Maryland

Shared Joy and Happiness

When schools work with students in a peak-performance zone driven by shared leadership, the result is shared joy and happiness. As described by Max De Pree, most successful organizations enjoy a common bond of interdependence, mutual interest, interlocking contributions, and simple joy. Part of the art of leadership is to ensure that this bond is maintained and strengthened. This is our goal at MGSD.

At MGSD, teachers take great pleasure and pride in students' success. They have told me hundreds of times that they love our students and think they are great, building a powerful sense of family and shared happiness. And the students are motivated to live up to their teachers' words of praise.

When students have teachers who smile and laugh with them, they feel connected to their teachers and want to learn from them and with them. When I was the principal of Northfield Elementary School in Tennessee, a second-grade boy told me, "We like to hear you laugh in our class, and Mrs. Duggin does too." Students love to laugh, and laughter helps to build bonds and overcome struggles.

LEADERSHIP VOICE

A Family of Colleagues

By **Felicia Bustle**
Principal, Mooresville Intermediate School

I have been very fortunate at MGSD to be surrounded by leaders who lead by example and from the heart. We are a family and share a mutual respect for one another.

Our executive director of elementary schools, Crystal Hill, has walked by my side from the day I began. She has mentored and encouraged me and modeled the type of leader I wanted to be. Scott Smith, our chief technology officer, has been gracious and supportive, setting expectations for our use of technology and modeling how the digital conversion should look. I learned a lot from Scott, not through directives and instructions, but on walkthroughs that we took together and from discussions of our observations.

I have taken the same approach with my own staff at Mooresville Intermediate School. We are a family here, too. I lead by example, and staff members know that I would never ask something of them that I would not be willing to do myself. We care for one another and treat each other with respect and dignity. We recognize that serious conversations may be needed at times, but always with the best interests of the students in mind.

Meeting Today's Challenges

Today's schools are facing multiple challenges that call for a new view of leadership. If we can rethink the traditional view that schools need only a few leaders at the top, we will be better positioned to meet those challenges and help our students succeed. I believe that high-performance teaching and learning driven by second-order, distributed leadership may be the only way to survive and thrive in many school districts today.

In order to address digital evolution, complex accountability standards, and shrinking budgets, we must develop strong leadership cultures to lift, pull, prod, cheer, and run with our teachers and staffs as they embrace their work and move toward high-performance teaching and learning.

Managing Change

School districts all over the United States are providing students and teachers with tablets or laptops and digital content, as we have done at MGSD, in the hope of enhancing teaching and learning. But many observers are urging caution because success rests on a multitude of factors beyond technology alone that interact and influence each other. (The interplay of MGSD success factors is outlined in my book *Every Child, Every Day*.)

Research suggests that one factor influencing success in this new environment is a deep understanding of change management and that change management requires leaders at all levels.

> **VISITOR FEEDBACK**   *"Less than one percent of the schools in the initial* Project RED *study met our standard success criteria. Highly complex new digital environments in schools must address the challenges of change management, and it takes leaders in lots of places to make that happen—in finance, technology, infrastructure, content, curriculum, classrooms, professional development, local community, and more."*
>
> —Tom Greaves, Jeanne Hayes,
> Leslie Wilson, Michael Gielniak, & Rick Peterson
> *The Technology Factor: Nine Keys to Student Achievement and Cost-Effectiveness*

At MGSD, we had to make some tough decisions and ultimately let some staff go. It is important to remember that carrying out the work of change management and leading transformation requires individual leadership and organizational backbone.

Serving the Community

At MGSD we believe in the importance of leadership development—for students as well as teachers. One example is the REACH Club, which gives young people the opportunity to work together in a world fellowship dedicated to service and international understanding. The objective is to develop initiative and leadership, to provide experience in living and working within a community, and to serve the school and community.

The club also helps students build GPAs, determine which courses to take for college, and fill out college applications. Students complete several service projects in the community each year to help improve their leadership skills.

LEADERSHIP VOICE

Going the Extra Mile

By **Samone Graham**
Mooresville High School Biology Teacher Leader, REACH Club Advisor, and Mooresville NAACP President

I grew up in Mooresville, and I remember when a lot of students who needed extra help did not get it. Today, everyone in the biology department has made a commitment to do whatever it takes to help every student, and we take turns to stay after school and offer tutoring sessions. We want every student to know that we care and we are just not going to let them fail.

When I got involved with the Mooresville NAACP, I told the officers that we have to reach out to students who might not have the support or role models at home. And that is exactly what we are doing. I am so proud of our students. They know that when we push them, we do it because we care.

Back when our graduation rate for minority students was in the 50 percent range, we all knew that was not acceptable, and when we hit 98 percent for African-American students, I could see the difference in the students' eyes. Every day we have to stay on it, and we will.

Doing More with Less

In our schools today, we are asking teachers, principals, superintendents, and school boards to do much more with less. In the new world of education, with its evolving accountability and funding challenges, schools need both broad and focused leadership to encourage staff to rise to the challenges and to provide training where needed.

At MGSD, the expectation is that every student in every class will be a successful learner, despite smaller budgets, larger class sizes, a more transient and changing community, and a constantly evolving digital conversion. Our staff has risen to the occasion, shown tremendous initiative, come up with new solutions to problems, and moved into new leadership roles.

Weathering the Storms

Our culture of distributed leadership helps us to weather ongoing storms. Leaders help everyone navigate a high-demand, high-expectation culture and face the challenges of complacency. This is hugely valuable in a time of ever tighter budgets.

LEADERSHIP IN ACTION

Initiative in Action

When our staff development funds were almost completely cut out of the budget, two teachers stepped up to the plate. Tracey Waid and Meghan McGrath became tech facilitators at Mooresville High School and Mooresville Middle School, respectively, providing much-needed support for staff learning in a time of funding challenges.

They became powerful leaders of both teachers and students. Working with individual teachers and teams, they now demonstrate how to use new digital content and model project- and inquiry-based learning methodologies. They also team teach with colleagues, helping them to learn on the job, and they offer a powerful collaborative learning model for students.

Tracey and Meghan are huge influencers who emerged as leaders when roles changed. Two other technology facilitators struggled with the changing demands of the job, but Tracey and Meghan embraced their roles as leaders, promoting innovation to the faculty and modeling collaboration. This change took time, but the result has been improved productivity, cost-effectiveness, and skills all around.

We have faced some tough times in terms of public education funding in North Carolina. Our teachers have not had a raise in five years, although we expect this situation will soon be remedied, and teacher morale in the state has dropped. At MGSD, teachers and staff lift each other up and cheer each other on, and this helps us face the challenges every day. Teachers, staff, and administrators step into their work with energy, enthusiasm, and passion.

A few years ago, we lost the funding to pay our teachers to stay after school and offer extra help sessions to students. Yet today we have more teachers offering more extra help sessions than ever before. Our teacher leaders are not only modeling leadership by their personal work but also encouraging others and organizing the work.

I am frequently asked how we "get" our teachers to tutor before and after school. I always reply that I don't "get" them to do what they do. They do it because they care, because they're committed, and because they are part of an "all in" culture that permeates every school.

And their dedication led to a new level of achievement for our district in 2014, when we reached more AMO (annual measurable objects) targets than any other district in the state, despite ranking only 100th in funding.

North Carolina AMO Targets Met, 2013–2014

AMO Targets Met Top 10 North Carolina Districts	% of Targets Met
1 Mooresville Graded School District	96.1
2 Union County	94.1
3 Polk County	93.5
4 Henderson County	92.9
5 Camden County	92.5
6 Mount Airy City	91.8
7 Watauga County	91.5
8 Carteret County	91.4
9 Dare County	91.3
10 Yancey County	91.1

AMO is based on students making a level 4 or 5 on EOG/EOC, EOG/EOC participation rate, math course rigor, graduation rate, ACT performance and participation rate, WorkKeys performance and participation rate, and attendance rate.

AMO = annual measurable objects, EOG = end-of-grade, EOC = end-of-course

Lasting Impact through Distributed Leadership

By **Dr. Aaron Spence**
Superintendent, Virginia Beach, Virginia, and Former Superintendent, Moore County Schools, North Carolina

One of the key challenges when implementing our digital learning initiative in Moore County was the need for buy-in and understanding. As a leader experienced with digital learning after working with Dr. Edwards in Henrico County, I was anxious to begin. However, I was also looking for long-term impact, and I knew that teachers had experienced a great deal of change, leading to widespread "initiative fatigue."

Most teachers in my district were willing to embrace the idea that digital learning could transform our schools, but few were eager to take on the practical work. So we recognized that an "all at once" approach was likely to fail, and we needed time to get comfortable with the new devices, instructional model, and procedures. We mapped out a plan that included multiple pilot sites.

I also knew that the initiative would fail if I was the only one who believed in it. So we identified principals who believed in the power of digital learning, and they volunteered to lead the pilot sites. They in turn identified teacher leaders who took on the initiative and ran with it in their classrooms. These pioneering leaders helped make the initiative work.

Because I had other projects that required my attention, I had to have a team of leaders at the district level that would give the pilot sites the support they needed. Several key leaders who believed in the vision took hold of it and operationalized every detail. Without them—especially the deputy superintendent, chief of technology, and lead technology coach—our digital learning initiative would never have found wings.

We distributed leadership amongst everyone who had a stake in the outcome, including teachers, principals, parents, students, and district administrators. I worked hard to establish a clear vision, but I also learned that lasting impact only comes with a flexible approach that lets those who have captured the vision step up and take a leading role to help realize it.

Custodian George Gardner receiving the 2013 Custodian of the Year award from Chris Gammon, assistant principal at Mooresville Intermediate School, watched by Todd Black, director of operations

When my son and I went over to Mooresville Intermediate School to play some basketball one rainy day last summer, we saw several custodians working in the cafeteria and stopped by to say hello. They were painstakingly working on the floor of the cafeteria to make sure it was spotless. "These corners are not easy to get clean, but we hit 'em a couple extra times, and we got 'em looking good," George Gardner said.

"I really appreciate the leadership each of you is showing as we prepare for our guests," I said. "Last year everyone said this school looked brand new, and your hard work is the reason why." I shook their hands and headed over to the gym.

REFLECTIVE QUESTIONS

1. What practical steps can you take toward distributed leadership?
2. How do you nurture the attitude that everyone's contribution is valuable?
3. What collective strategies can you implement to address problems?
4. How can you encourage the concept of roving leaders?
5. How do you support change management thinking?

REFERENCES

Edwards, Mark. (2014). *Every Child, Every Day*. Upper Saddle River, NJ: Pearson Education.

De Pree, Max. (1990). *Leadership Is an Art*. New York, NY: Dell.

Greaves, Tom; Hayes, Jeanne; Wilson, Leslie; Gielniak, Michael; & Peterson, Rick. (2010). *The Technology Factor: Nine Keys to Student Achievement and Cost-Effectiveness*. Sheldon, CT: MDR.

Chapter 2

Leaders with a Shared Vision

"The presence of leaders is felt everywhere in our district, providing support and direction at every turn."

On a visit to the Mooresville & Mebane Summer Literacy Lift, I explained to our guests that they would be seeing several different kinds of MGSD leaders in action. The institute provided a summer literacy program for first- through third-grade students with reading deficiencies, partially funded by the Mebane Foundation. We began the visit by meeting Dr. Crystal Hill, MGSD Executive Director of Elementary Education, who had led the development of the program.

She introduced us to the program director, Cheryl Dortch, MGSD 2011 Teacher of the Year, and together we visited the second-grade class. Here we met a young teacher, Lauren Wally, the Beginning Teacher of the Year at Rocky River Elementary School, who was on the floor helping three boys write stories on their iPads.

In the next room, a group of students was working on a reading assignment led by A'Lishia Bowman, a rising sophomore at Mooresville High School and a student mentor/tutor. A'Lishia was an excellent leader for these students since she lived in their neighborhood, and they obviously wanted to please her and meet her expectations.

The next classroom was filled with students doing research on animals, led by Troy Eckles, a recent Mooresville High School graduate who was working as a student tutor for the summer before heading off to Howard University. Cheryl told us what a great role model Troy was for these students and how they looked up to him.

The smiles and enthusiasm all around were remarkable and clearly influencing student progress, as each leader proudly led his or her area of responsibility.

I believe that a high level of encouragement by a wide range of leaders—each addressing a different area of leadership, supporting each other, and getting to know students as individuals—is an essential factor in continually building student and teacher success.

Our digital conversion initiative is like a river that constantly changes course as it flows along, so we are always adapting to new dynamic content and accountability policies. As we navigate the bends in the river, many leaders are needed to support our staff and maintain the focus on moving forward—for students, departments, schools, and the district as a whole. So we have integrated distributed leadership into every facet of our work, and we have supported leadership development by focusing on coaching and collaboration, believing that success for our students is directly tied to our relentless support and coaching of staff.

At MGSD, leaders work together to create a synergy that is a real force in our day-to-day activity. We have pushed the work of leadership out beyond the administrator level so that we have leaders all around us—working, giving, caring, learning, sharing, and leading. The presence of leaders is felt everywhere in our district, providing support and direction at every turn.

Last year CoSN brought leadership teams from 23 school districts to see the digital conversion that has happened in Mooresville and then spark a conversation in other districts about how to scale similar transformation.

VISITOR FEEDBACK *"Perhaps the most powerful part of the entire experience was hearing from the Mooresville leadership team—from Dr. Edwards to the heads of curriculum, technology, and finance. They literally could finish each other's sentences. It was much more than having one strong leader, and clearly Dr. Edwards is a strong leader. Rather, we saw that the Mooresville team had formed with a common vision. That was distributed leadership in action."*

—Keith Krueger
Chief Executive Officer, CoSN (Consortium for School Networking)

Principals and Assistant Principals

Research has shown that principals have a huge impact on the quality of schools, and many observers have suggested that every great school has a great principal. As a superintendent for over 20 years, I have worked with principals in three different school systems, and I believe that the research is accurate. I can say with certainty that the many great principals I have worked with have had a huge impact not only on schools but also on lives and communities.

Principals and assistant principals do complex and challenging work and play a huge role in the daily lives of schools. At MGSD, our principals and assistant principals have grown enormously. They are constantly learning new skills and leadership strategies in their daily quest for excellence.

Developing Other Leaders

In a digital conversion initiative with a distributed leadership model, formal leaders must lead with new skills. One of their most important new skills is nurturing leadership in others as they actively develop teacher and staff leaders.

Our principals understand that the result of this effort, when teacher leaders influence and lead their colleagues, is an uplift effect across all areas of school life that directly impacts student achievement. Because best practices are always emerging and evolving as we implement new digital content, we need a lot of leaders in a lot of places. As teacher leaders share best practices and "coach up" other teachers, they help to build an instructional synergy that improves student learning and teacher effectiveness.

Dee Gibbs, the principal of N. F. Woods Advanced Technology and Arts Center, always calls on his department chairs to lead at quarterly information meetings. Under his inspirational leadership, his staff has embraced the important mission of relentlessly championing the students who need our help the most. He leads our Mi-Waye alternative school program, serving about 60 students who are finding a path to graduation that includes credit recovery and small classes, with tremendous support from the staff. Many Mi-Waye students have struggled with academics, discipline, and other issues.

Mr. Gibbs also works with local business leaders in our Career Bridge Advisory, to help students find opportunities with local businesses and raise money to support students who make it to national competitions. In 2014, 17 students were involved in national competitions, and we had plenty of resources to fund the travel for students and staff.

Leadership development is not limited to the teaching staff. When I visit our schools with the principals, I always hear them acknowledge the work of others. On a visit to the Park View Elementary cafeteria staff, the principal, Mark Cottone, told me, "These ladies have got to be the best staff we have here at MGSD. Every day they come in with enthusiasm and kindness for our students and make a difference."

Leadership Development in Action

A few years ago, we hired a new dietician, Kim McCall, for our school food service program. With the support of our CFO, Terry Haas, who is responsible for the child nutrition program, Kim soon provided leadership regarding nutritional standards and menu development.

Then she went one step further and started sending out fun emails every day with tips for healthy living. As a result, several faculty and teacher leaders initiated and participated in healthy living activities, including exercise classes, Weight Watchers groups, and walking clubs. Kim is respected and constantly learning along with her staff, who like her style.

Every good principal invests heavily in the development of teacher and staff leaders. Many of our cafeteria staff, bus drivers, custodians, and office staff have evolved as leaders with the help, encouragement, and direction of others and now model daily excellence in their work and attitudes. Interwoven in the leadership culture of all MGSD administrators is the daily work of affirming leaders and the great work of students, teachers, staff, parents, and everyone else who is part of the MGSD family.

Modeling the Importance of Learning

Our principals function as role models for everyone else by working on their own learning. Most have completed or are completing their doctoral degrees, and they support others who are working on degrees or additional certifications. They also help plan and lead professional development on our early release days.

As part of our professional development program, we use a book study format every year to further our understanding of leadership work. In 2013, the study group discussion of *Leadership Is an Art* by Max De Pree was led by three principals—Mark Cottone of Park View Elementary, Jason Gardner of East Mooresville Intermediate, and Dee Gibbs of N. F. Woods—along with one assistant principal, Angelo DelliSanti of Mooresville Middle School.

They developed an interactive small-group activity that kept everyone highly engaged as we discussed the different ways we could weave De Pree's concepts into our own work. I love to see this kind of professional development session because it shows leaders influencing others and growing in their own skills.

Interestingly, in 2013 Mark had just completed his doctoral work in one of our cohorts with Wingate University, and Jason and Angelo were doctoral candidates in a new cohort. It was clear that their formal adult learning programs were greatly enhancing their work as school leaders.

How Leaders Model Learning

- Stay engaged.
- Talk to students and staff about their work.
- Encourage, acknowledge, and smile.
- Ask questions and want to know.
- Work hard to help others.
- Coach with conviction.
- Lead with purpose, energy, enthusiasm, and focus.
- Share with others what they are learning.
- Continue their personal learning journey.

Maintaining Visibility

I strongly believe that students and staff need to see their principals all the time and that the leadership presence of principals influences collaboration and learning. At MGSD, principals do not stay in their offices for a good part of the day, as they do in some schools. They roam around the building, in and out of classrooms, in the cafeteria, in the hallways, and on the grounds. They work on the go, and they make things go.

They lead by their presence and their effort, as they observe and influence the daily flow of student and teacher work. Some of their most important work kicks in when they encourage a student, acknowledge a teacher, or share their observations about leadership with someone else.

Assistant principals are also a significant part of our leadership fabric. Like principals, they are highly visible to students and staff at all times, providing leadership in all aspects of our work and adding value for students, staff, and parents.

When I walk through a school with a principal, students almost always approach him or her to ask for advice, confess about homework, or share a success. The personal presence of principals is very important to them.

Visibility in Action

MGSD principals and assistant principals are literally "out front" in our leadership effort, meeting students and parents on the sidewalk every morning. Parents love to see a smiling professional greet their children by name, and we use this opportunity to communicate that each day is a new day to learn. Our goal is to transform what many schools view as a routine task into a way to lead and set the tone.

"I know it's a little thing, but when our principal Mr. Gardner is standing out front, opening car doors, and saying good morning, I just love it. It gives us all a sense of security," commented Lisa Gill, PTO leader and mother of three MGSD students.

Similarly, teachers, custodians, bus drivers, and others need to hear a supportive "good morning, and we're counting on you" message every day from their principals and assistant principals, acknowledging that they are valued team players in the work of educating students.

Jason Gardner, the principal at East Mooresville Intermediate School, focuses much of his energy and effort on knowing and interacting with students. When I walk through his school with him, in class after class students call out to him to come and look at their work or their results. It is powerful to see the personal connection he has forged with students.

A few years ago, while visiting a school, I noticed that few if any students interacted with the principal on our classroom visits. I shared with her that she needed to become more engaged with students, and on a recent visit I saw that she had taken the feedback to heart. Dozens of kids had comments for her, hugged her, and talked to her as we walked through the school.

Using the Data

To meet our performance goals, we rely on principals to lead in the use of formative data, working with teacher leaders to constantly adjust the instructional focus and maximize the use of digital resources. We expect our principals to develop teacher leaders to support this work by continually reviewing data with teachers and aligning instruction to meet the needs of students. The continual

MGSD Quarterly Math Results, by Fourth-Grade Teacher

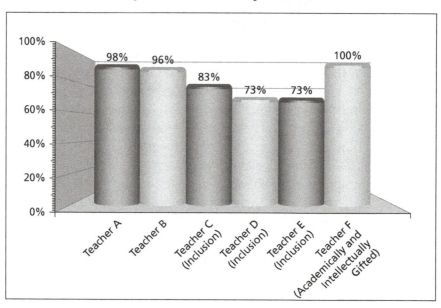

work of calibrating instruction—by teacher, department, and student—is vital to school success and takes full advantage of the data resources available through digital conversion.

Dr. Carrie Tulbert, principal of Mooresville Middle School, always focuses intensely on analyzing data with the department leaders in her school. Through her leadership, her faculty culture has shifted from "we're doing what we have to do" to "we are a cadre of teacher leaders who view formative data as a vital component of student achievement and are willing to lead others in the effort." The difference in attitude has had a huge impact on instruction.

Setting a Caring Tone

To create the right context for teaching and learning, our principals encourage, acknowledge, and direct as they go about their day. When I visit schools with them, they generally share a few comments about each teacher as we move from class to class. In most cases, they acknowledge some special effort the teacher or the class has made.

In the spring of 2013, when I visited South Elementary School with the principal, Debbie Marsh, she said to me as we entered Hayley Johnson's

Caring in Action

At one of our information meetings, Principal Dee Gibbs told us, "Our teachers have identified the students who need special encouragement. I'm getting together with them in small groups to let them know we care about them, and we're going to stay with them."

Teacher Ashley Ericson confirmed the value of this personal attention. "Mr. Gibbs has been meeting with three young men who have to get it together if they're going to graduate," she said. "I know they're listening to him because they're asking me if they're caught up. One has a terrible home life, and I know Mr. Gibbs has been encouraging him and has brought him some clothes."

second-grade class, "I want you to know I'm so proud of Hayley. She's our grade-level chair. Although she's a young teacher, she has really stepped up her game and is providing strong leadership."

As I shook Hayley's hand, I repeated Dr. Marsh's words to her and congratulated her on jumping into the role of grade-level chair. She beamed back at me but immediately turned to help a student pulling at her sleeve. Dr. Marsh's acknowledgment of her leadership and the leadership of others impacts the success of students at South Elementary every day.

Dee Gibbs, the veteran principal at the N. F. Woods Advanced Technology and Arts Center, a sister school to Mooresville High School that hosts our CTE (Career and Technical Education) and alternative Mi-Waye programs, sets the tone by supporting the students who struggle the most and always letting them know that someone cares.

Teacher Leaders

Almost every visitor to MGSD comments on our teacher leaders—our department chairs and our elementary and middle school grade-level chairs—who do great work with students and peers in every school. They set an example for their colleagues and are "in the trenches" every day, encouraging and offering advice and direction.

They are also important members of our interview committees when we are looking to hire new teachers, principals, and assistant principals. This model aligns with Daniel Pink's work on motivation in *Drive: The Surprising Truth about What Motivates Us*, which indicates that teachers need to have a major voice in how they achieve goals, design instruction, and conduct their professional work. And I believe we make better hiring decisions as a result of their participation.

Teacher leaders who have a voice embrace accountability and work with challenges because they know it's up to them. As Roland Barth stresses in *Learning by Heart*, empowerment and collaborative learning are essential for the betterment of the teaching profession.

Teacher leaders must be willing to embrace a leadership role in order to help their colleagues learn and grow, as well as to learn and grow themselves. As Sharon Markofski, the Mooresville High School math department chair, told me a few years ago, "We don't need any lone rangers. We all have to pitch in, work together, and learn from each other to make this work."

In April 2014, on a visit to Mooresville Middle School, I walked in and out of classrooms with the principal, Carrie Tulbert, sharing a running dialogue about the work of teachers and teams and how it was going. She told me that she had asked social studies teacher Jeff Wright to lead one of the grade-level teams, and he had really stepped up, despite his initial doubts about his ability to lead.

Mr. Wright's growth in the digital conversion had not always come easy, but he plugged away to build his skills and effectiveness. Dr. Tulbert's expectation that each

LEADERSHIP IN ACTION

Change Leadership in Action

Mike Micklow, the boys' basketball coach at Mooresville High School, was an early adopter and leader in our digital conversion. Coach Micklow loves developing basketball players, but he also loves developing students' math skills, particularly their algebra skills.

Teaching math in a digital environment was challenging for some teachers at first, but Mike led them in successfully adapting to the change. He showed them how to enhance math problems with visual elements from the software program *Comic Life*, giving students more engaging examples and a new way to look at math problems.

faculty member will evolve and her nurturing of those who need a little more time have paid off. It is important to note that the changes required by MGSD's digital conversion and every child, every day culture were extremely challenging for many staff, and it has taken several years to build the cultural acumen that we now enjoy.

Our belief in teacher leaders and our high expectations for them helps to increase their contribution to improving outcomes for our students and is a major part of our school and district culture. Bolman and Deal describe this phenomenon in *Leading with Soul:*

> "Trusting people to solve problems generates higher levels of motivation and better solutions. The leader's responsibility is to create conditions that promote authorship. Individuals need to see their work as meaningful and worthwhile, to feel personally accountable for the consequences of their efforts, and to get feedback that lets them know the results."

Leading Staff Development

Our department and grade-level chairs as well as other teacher leaders plan and lead staff development programs, providing support and encouragement for new staff. They implement much of the training and reflective analysis on the 10 early release days a year that we dedicate to professional development.

Our instructional technology facilitators at each school now train others on how to navigate alignment with new state accountability standards and assessments and implement the features and functionality of new digital content. Their contribution has evolved way beyond running computer labs. They play a major role in supporting the growth of their colleagues in our digital conversion.

Digital conversion requires that pedagogy continuously evolve along with online content, and our teacher leaders play a key role in making this happen. We arrange for new teachers to observe them so that they can see how the teacher leaders organize instruction to maximize collaboration and digital resources.

Over time, we have developed a cadre of professional development mentors who are great teachers not only of students but also of colleagues. It only makes sense in our schools, at MGSD and nationwide, to tap into the phenomenal resource of teaching expertise to develop the skills of other staff.

Learning from each other has led to a shared sense of exhilaration and an evolving esprit de corps at MGSD. Unlike the traditional leadership model, distributed leadership builds connections among staff members that inspire them in their daily work with students.

Leading Data Analysis

At each MGSD school, teacher leaders have become skilled at using information to align instructional support to student needs, and their local leadership boosts the engine that drives student achievement. They help to analyze student formative data, implement instructional adjustments, and coach other staff.

In our quarterly information meetings, we review a profile of each course, break it down by student and subgroup, and look at the content areas for specific strengths and needs. Our teacher leaders proactively follow up on the results of these reviews.

Championing Change

MGSD's digital conversion initiative requires that we constantly learn new software and adapt to a changing instructional model. We have looked to our

---

LEADERSHIP IN ACTION

Data Analysis in Action

At a recent information meeting, Ashley Ericson, the business department chair at N. F. Woods Advanced Technology and Arts Center, outlined the following plan: "We've looked at the data and identified every student who needs help, and we're asking the parents to encourage their children to come to tutoring sessions before or after school. We know if we can get them here, we can get them up to speed. We have to bear down at times, but we're on the right track."

I'm always impressed by the N. F. Woods teachers' laser focus on data. Their data analysis skills, inspiring leadership, and caring attitude have translated into great success for students. In spring of 2013 and spring of 2014, a dozen students from this school won state championships and made it to the national finals in CTE skill competitions. N. F. Woods also achieved its highest-ever composite score on the North Carolina VoCATS Assessments, a 92 percent pass rate.

Briona Rivers and Monica Phutthavong, CTE students and North Carolina State Champions in the Life Event Planning section of Family Career and Community Leaders of America, with board chair Larry Wilson and their sponsor Donna Poynton

teacher leaders to be champions of change in this effort while focusing on skill development for every student. And we have observed that champions and leaders sometimes emerge in unexpected places. When schools embrace a culture of distributed leadership, they benefit from a wide range of skills and experience, so we look for leadership everywhere.

Mooresville Middle School English teacher Bethany Smith helped lead the curricular and methodology change with digital conversion, and today she leads sessions at our Summer Connection Institute, showing educators from all over the country that teachers can make English more appealing to students and do a highly effective job in a digital, project-based, and collaborative environment.

Roseann Burklow, another teacher at Mooresville Middle School, did not initially embrace the change. But later "the lights came on" for Roseann. It took her a couple of years to move from complying with the changes to embracing them, but she has been soaring ever since. She now leads professional development sessions for MGSD and other districts and was recently honored with the prestigious DEN Award from Discovery Education.

My Journey from Textbooks to Computers

By **Roseann Burklow**
Fifth-Grade Science Teacher,
Mooresville Intermediate School

When our digital conversion started in 2007, I was a 25-year teaching veteran. Needless to say, I was very comfortable with my science textbook, paper, and pencil, and I had no idea I was about to embark on the most challenging, yet rewarding journey of my career.

My first "aha" moment came back in 2007, when I created my first digital lesson, and I saw my students have fun learning again. I started to see that they were blossoming into young scientists, eager to research, collaborate, connect to the real world, and take ownership of their learning. Also, I realized that technology provided easy tools to plan lessons for differentiation and review. Thanks to the training, support, and encouragement I received from everyone, I was soon able to step out of my comfort zone and make the cultural shift to a technology-driven classroom.

Now, seven years later, I have created and shared many digital lessons and activities with my fellow teachers throughout the district and beyond. Every year, I continue to grow and learn about new websites and programs. I always find it exciting to implement them in the classroom and watch student engagement grow.

I am grateful for the opportunity I was given to shift into the 21st century right along with my students, to revel in their success, and to become a better teacher.

Planning and Leading Conferences

MGSD's teacher leaders, principals, and central office staff join together to plan and lead our Summer Connection Conference for other districts, on how to implement a digital conversion, and our Summer Institute for MGSD teachers, on how to implement new software, build collaborative teams, and grow along with students.

They have fully embraced this responsibility. Working together to design developmental constructs for peers and each other, they have raised the level of their own knowledge and commitment. (Please see Appendix C and Appendix D for sample conference agendas.)

Central Office Leaders

MGSD's central office team leads by example as they constantly offer service to teachers, principals, staff, parents, and each other. Terry Haas, chief financial officer, focuses all her efforts on helping others find a way to get the job done in a very difficult budget climate—not an easy task.

She has also shown leadership in a personal context. She lost 50 pounds, transformed her health, and helped develop a new online personal wellness program for voluntary district implementation. Our digital conversion is everywhere!

Terry Haas and Tanae McLean, our public information officer, are our main event planners and leaders, whether it's a visit from President Obama or the meals for the Summer Connection Conference. Tanae worked 14 hours a day for weeks before the president's visit, modeling for others how to step up and lead as the situation required.

Scott Smith, our chief technical officer, constantly triangulates his work with our executive directors of instruction, Crystal Hill and Steve Mauney, to maximize efficiency, influence teaching and learning, and model caring for all employees. Crystal and Steve model focus, energy, compassion, and the need to keep student learning on the front burner at all times. Because we have a very small central office team, our key instructional leaders juggle many responsibilities every day as they provide targeted leadership to our principals.

The results are strong personal relationships and connections across the board. When Scott Smith's mother passed away unexpectedly a few years ago, the entire central office administration team drove to Greensboro, a couple of hours away, to support him at the service.

Todd Black, our director of operations, who joined the team in 2012, said at a recent principals' meeting, "I knew MGSD had a great team, but every day I'm amazed and motivated by the leadership synergy here. Now I want to mobilize every member of the operations team to build on the synergy and take the game up even higher."

Leaders must be attentive to caring for others. According to Bolman and Deal in *Leading with Soul*, "The heart of leadership resides in the hearts of leaders." My observation during 20 years as a superintendent is that every high-performance central office leader combines exacting leadership with an outstanding work ethic and deep compassion for others.

> **VISITOR FEEDBACK** *"At MGSD, I have seen leaders moving together, shoulder to shoulder, each committed to a commonly shared mission and set of described outcomes. Mooresville has shown us that it is possible to do more with less while encouraging each leader to rediscover why he or she chose to become a professional educator. It is not about heaping the load on a few but gladly sharing the burden across many aligned, passionate leaders."*
>
> —Randy Wilhelm
> Chief Executive Officer, Knovation

Student Leaders

Many years ago, I thought of student leadership primarily in terms of the high school student council or other groups where students assume formal leadership roles. However, I have developed a new point of view over the years, after watching students exhibit leadership from kindergarten through high school and college. I've developed a new appreciation for the important role of student leadership in advancing learning and productivity.

Every year, MGSD students open the Summer Connection Conference with presentations and conversations about their personal experience in the digital conversion. These young leaders, from fifth graders to seniors, always dazzle the audience with their insights and work samples. As you might expect, they offer many examples of digital learning, including multimedia projects and collaborative mashups of student research.

Emerging Collaborative Model

In MGSD's digital conversion initiative, project-based work is a vital part of our instructional framework, and we have fully integrated students to help lead the learning process. We encourage students at all grade levels to work together on projects where they are given leadership assignments and expected to navigate and thrive while leading others.

Meghan McGrath, assistant principal at East Mooresville Intermediate School, encouraging a student before his presentation at the 2014 Summer Connection Conference

Student Leadership in Action

When I was the superintendent in Henrico County, Virginia, I was standing in the foyer of Laburnum Elementary School with the principal, Mr. Gunn, when we saw a five or six-year-old boy hurrying up the sidewalk with just a t-shirt on, despite the December rain. He was holding something we couldn't quite make out. He came inside, oblivious to the cold and rain, and proudly held out a can of food, saying, "Mr. Gunn, my momma said we could give this can of beans for the poor kids."

Mr. Gunn thanked him, and the boy smiled brightly and went off to class. "William's family is the very first on the list of needy families we're collecting for," said Mr. Gunn. We both stood for a few minutes knowing that William had just shown us a great example of student leadership.

We utilize instructional design models throughout the grades, where students teach each other new software features or science and math concepts. Even elementary students coach and encourage each other in paired reading activities. We tap into an emerging collaborative learning model that both requires and leverages student leadership as part of the design.

We as educators still have a long way to go to fully realize the potential of this powerful model and consistently utilize student leaders as part of the instructional design, but this is an important goal we need to focus on in the coming years.

LEADERSHIP VOICE

Students Training Students

By **Mary Royal**
Counselor, Mooresville Middle School

At one of our school improvement team meetings, we decided to set up training groups, led by "veteran" students, for middle school students who were new to the district. Since I was new to the middle school grade levels, I was a little hesitant to go with student-led rather than counselor-led groups, but we decided to solicit student names from the staff, and we gave about 20 veteran students a challenge-based learning opportunity.

We asked them to take responsibility for 60 new students and help them become familiar with Keynote, Pages, iMovie, Angel, and Mac shortcuts. With a little guidance, they split into "centers," and each volunteered to take charge of a different application.

The following Friday, we ran three sessions where rookie students rotated in and out of the room to learn about the most frequently used MacBook applications at Mooresville Middle School. The veteran students did very well. They split into small groups, shared mini-presentations with the new students, fielded questions, and led discussions on how to best utilize the MacBooks in class. I was impressed.

However, I noticed that two girls had totally separated themselves from the groups and were sitting at a table alone and in silence, staring at their screens. I observed them from across the room for a few minutes and wondered if they were doing homework or perhaps even playing games. The rest of the students were chatting, moving around, and switching laptops to show off their knowledge.

I quietly walked up behind the two girls and peeked over their shoulders, and what I saw gave me goose bumps. They were using Google Translate to communicate. One girl spoke only Spanish and was typing questions in Spanish into the program. The other girl spoke only English and was using the program to translate her answers into Spanish. The Spanish-speaking girl later returned to her ESL classroom and excitedly showed her teacher all the questions and answers and all the new things that she had learned.

This is a tribute to our students and how much they can accomplish with a little freedom and trust when they are encouraged to take on a leadership role. It was also a learning experience for me. Any doubts I had had about the student-led groups were gone.

Peer Instruction

We at MGSD see peer instruction and project collaboration as a means to fully embrace a basic fact about student learning—that students will always learn from each other. From second grade on, we encourage students to share with each other what they have just learned and how they learned it. This transfer of knowledge is very powerful.

Whether it's AP chemistry or second-grade math, we deliberately include shared learning and collaboration as vital tools in our instructional design. Small groups and peer-to-peer instruction give students the opportunity to lead others and reinforce their own knowledge at the same time.

TEAM One

At Mooresville High School, math chair Sharon Markofski and a colleague took the initiative a couple years ago to introduce a concept they call TEAM One (Total Efficacy for Achieving More One) to administrative leaders. Their idea was to develop a group of student leaders to provide peer instruction in math to rising ninth graders who had been identified as possible dropouts based on their academics, attendance, behavior, or home life struggles, and then to ramp up a summer program to build their capacity to succeed and lead. TEAM One now meets throughout the year to foster collegial connections among students and staff.

TEAM One is designed to help students during their freshman year. Targeted students are incoming freshmen whose math EVAAS (Education Value-Added Assessment System) scores are less than 55 percent proficient, who were recommended by their eighth-grade teachers for extra help, and who want to achieve more through learning and hard work.

TEAM One students are invited to attend a June summer session for a positive first experience on the high school campus. A structured learning environment is provided through work in ELA (English Language Arts) and mathematics. Foundations of Algebra is incorporated into the curriculum to prepare students for the Math 1 course they will take the second semester. The primary goal is to close learning gaps.

TEAM One Courses

- Study skills
- Organization skills
- Leadership skills
- Collaborative skills
- 21st-century skills, including technology
- North Carolina higher standards Math 1 skills

TEAM One Activities

- Team building/collaboration
- Career-ready investigations with community/business partners
- College visits to two- and four-year schools
- Business and professional speakers
- Tutoring

AP Student Leaders

MGSD high school student leaders are committed to helping others advance their vertical progression and logical understanding of mathematics, with high-achieving students helping those who are trying to close learning gaps. The AP

Peer Instruction in Action

On a visit to Sharon Markofski's math class, a TEAM One student leader explained to me, "Today we're making iMovies of each other demonstrating how to do problems, and then we're sharing them. Other kids can use them at home or here if they need to see how to do it again. I'm going to make sure my friend here can do these problems on any test." He smiled at his fellow student and placed a hand on his shoulder.

calculus students begin working with Math 1 students as soon as the AP exams are over in early May, to help their peers achieve success on their end-of-course exam.

AP students report to an assigned Math 1 teacher, who structures the peer tutoring of Math 1 students. The AP students learn appropriate questioning techniques, hints to prompt further thinking, and technology tools that support deeper understanding of core concepts. During help sessions, they offer one-to-one peer instruction to help Math 1 students learn the concepts and testing strategies.

Tutoring is held in a flexible and comfortable environment, sometimes in the Math 1 classroom, sometimes on the floor in the hallway, and sometimes in another teacher's room. AP students debrief with the teacher after the sessions so that they can reflect on and improve their tutoring practice to meet individual needs.

The students build strong bonds, with caring and compassion in evidence as new friendships build character and work ethic. Both groups of math students benefit by learning many life lessons while coming together to complete the math cycle with continuous alignment and support. As we say at Mooresville High School, it's "blue devil helping blue devil."

Support Staff

In most school districts, about half of the employees are support staff—bus drivers, custodians, food service workers, maintenance workers, clerical staff, and technical support staff. This group is naturally very influential because it is so large, but unfortunately many districts fail to acknowledge this powerful force and do not fully benefit from the contributions of these individuals, although these staff can play a huge role in helping students, families, and teachers get the support they need.

Maintenance worker Roger Lambert, pruning roses

Authors Max De Pree, Michael Fullan, and Roland Barth emphasize that all members of the school culture are essential for organizational success, and Margaret Wheatley points to the idea that each staff member is both symbiotic with the rest of the organization and part of the whole.

In MGSD, we have seen magnificent leadership emerge from the ranks of our support staff. Roger Lambert, one of our maintenance staff, is a true leader who works extremely hard. Among many other things, Roger and his colleagues keep our grounds looking great. Roger took the initiative to put rose bushes around each school sign, and when President Obama came to visit Mooresville Middle School, the sign was adorned with beautiful roses.

Some MGSD bus drivers not only greet each student with a personal hello each morning but also get to know the kids and parents. They support students with a caring attitude on the way to and from school every day. Our cafeteria staff greet students by name and often know their personal food choices.

Our entire central office staff, including my administrative assistant, Jean Millsaps, provide responsive service to all and know that their communication and leadership skills are important to each school's success. When I visit schools, I make a point of thanking our support staff with a handshake and a smile. I used to thank them for their hard work, and now I thank many for their leadership.

LEADERSHIP IN ACTION

All-Around Leadership in Action

Mooresville High School English teacher and boys' tennis coach Tim Smith helped create a "varsity club" to provide community service. The club decided to support local autistic students in an elementary soccer league, with club members and autistic students paired up together.

At the end-of-season picnic, when Coach Smith spoke about the outstanding job the high school students had done, Brad Gandy, our maintenance HVAC specialist, brought out his grill and helped cook hot dogs and hamburgers for the players, coaches, and varsity club members. He showed outstanding leadership, as did the students, Coach Smith, and the autistic students, who stepped up with courage and determination to try something new.

School Board, Parents, and Community

I have worked with some excellent school board members during my career, and we are fortunate in Mooresville to have school board members who truly believe in our mission of every child, every day. They take their leadership role very seriously, model teamwork, and are highly engaged.

MGSD school board members have demonstrated leadership by introducing early release days for professional development, which has been central to the success of our digital conversion. Board members have high expectations, and they are vocal cheerleaders for our students and the entire staff.

Our parent advisory committees are also an important component of our leadership work. Each school identifies and recruits 8 to 12 parent leaders, along with other leaders from band and athletic boosters and other organizations, to serve on the parent advisory board and attend quarterly and other occasional meetings. Feedback and advice about our digital conversion are on the agenda at every meeting. Parent leaders have advised on a wide range of topics, from parent training to backpack selection.

Our parent and community leaders also take a strong stand when it comes to support for educational funding and other issues related to our schools. The Mooresville Education Foundation and the Career Bridge Foundation, which supports our CTE programs, include many local business leaders who offer tremendous support to our schools and programs.

Our mayor, police chief, and several other elected leaders are involved with our district and offer formal leadership support. Our chamber of commerce and economic development leaders work closely with us on the shared goal of building opportunity in the community. I believe that all school districts can reap dividends by cultivating collaboration and leadership among parents and community members.

LEADERSHIP VOICE

Broad Benefits to the Community

By **Miles Atkins**
Mayor, Mooresville, North Carolina

The Mooresville community has benefitted immensely from the changes in our school system. The district has leveled the learning playing field by giving every child equal access to educational resources and tools. And a partnership with our municipally owned broadband system is providing basic Internet service at no charge to families of children who receive free or reduced-price meals. For Mooresville's underserved population, this has been a huge plus.

In addition, families are relocating to Mooresville from all over the country because of the reputation of our schools, and the increased demand for housing has fueled a housing boom in our town. Our business community recognizes that our schools play a key role in talent recruitment, and the district has formed strong alliances with our top employers, who have become great supporters. My office and the city council are tremendous supporters of MGSD. The Chamber of Commerce and the Economic Development Commission work in partnership with MGSD to leverage the work of our students and schools and position our town for economic development and positive growth.

The district is not only a community partner that contributes to our sense of place, it is also an economic engine driving an emerging edutourism industry, as hundreds of educators from around the country attend the MGSD Summer Connection Conference, filling our hotels for a week and spending their free time in our downtown. In addition, teachers, researchers, and education industry executives visit Mooresville throughout the year, contributing to an educational innovation hub that benefits all our citizens.

My office is working with our school district to create a hub of educational excellence, innovation, entrepreneurship, and technology that enjoys national recognition. We are proud that the president of the United States, the secretary of education, and the governor of North Carolina have all visited our town and acknowledged the innovation in our schools.

At one of our Summer Connection Conferences, a Mooresville Middle School student who had recently transferred from New York and was struggling with a number of issues, addressed the audience. "Hello, I'm Juan from Mooresville Middle School, and I'm going to show you my architectural design project," he said. "When I did this project, I discovered a couple of things about myself and a couple of other important things. First, I discovered I love architectural design, and I'm good at it." He shared his impressive 3D design on the screen projected from his school laptop.

"Last year I dropped out of school," he continued. "I'm a year behind because my family moves around a lot, and we've had some problems. But the principal and my counselor came to see me and my mom, and they said I just couldn't drop out. And that was that. So I'm going to Mooresville High School next year, and I can't wait to start drafting class. I learned you have to believe in yourself, and it's great to have a principal and counselor and teachers who care about you. Thank you." The ovation lasted a long time as this young leader returned to his seat.

REFLECTIVE QUESTIONS

1. How do you develop a shared vision among all leaders?

2. How can you consciously work on setting the tone in your district?

3. Do you acknowledge the leadership contributions of support staff?

4. What are some nontraditional ways you can encourage students to become leaders?

5. What leadership opportunities are available to your teachers outside the classroom?

REFERENCES

Barth, Roland S. (2001). *Learning by Heart.* San Francisco, CA: Jossey-Bass.

Bolman, Lee G., & Deal, Terrence E. (2011). *Leading with Soul: An Uncommon Journey of Spirit.* San Francisco, CA: Jossey-Bass.

De Pree, Max. (1990). *Leadership Is an Art.* New York, NY: Dell.

Fullan, Michael. (2010). *All Systems Go: The Change Imperative for Whole System Reform.* Thousand Oaks, CA: Corwin.

Pink, Daniel H. (2009). *Drive: The Surprising Truth about What Motivates Us.* New York, NY: Riverhead Books.

Wheatley, Margaret. (2006). *Leadership and the New Science: Discovering Order in a Chaotic World.* San Francisco, CA: Berrett-Koehler.

Chapter 3

Aligning Leaders with the Mission

"The alignment of leaders with a school or district mission has huge implications for successful innovation."

Visitors to MGSD often comment that everyone is on the same page, and in 2014, I witnessed this alignment during some discussions about instructional improvement strategies at our winter information meetings. Teacher leaders at each school described how the teams had worked together to vet formative data and how they planned to use the data to align class work with students' individual and collective needs.

"We know where we need to focus and adjust the interventions," said Maureen Fitzsimmons, math department chair at Mooresville Middle School. "The new standards [the North Carolina Common Core Standards and Assessments] are tough, and it will take time to adjust, but we are all over it together, and we will get it right."

The alignment of leaders with a school or district mission has huge implications for successful innovation. Alignment in schools is a lot like alignment in cars. When cars are out of alignment, you can feel it and sometimes even see it, but when they are in alignment, the ride is smooth.

Educators generally think of alignment in terms of curriculum, but at MGSD we take a much broader view. Although curriculum alignment is essential, we also work at aligning leadership development, professional development, resource allocation, and communication with our mission. This is a complex task but one we work at every day, in order to develop the synergy to improve teaching and learning throughout the system.

Ongoing Work of Alignment

The tight alignment of MGSD leaders with the mission did not happen overnight. It was built over several years, as principals, assistant principals, teacher leaders, and central office leaders participated in an ever-evolving discussion about our focus on the success of every student.

This work never ends and requires constant attention. It is the work of everyone, every day. At MGSD we have worked hard to consistently align our leadership capacity with a common vision—our mission of every child, every day—and we systematically connect everything we do to our main goal.

When everyone takes responsibility for alignment, everyone has the power to chart a trajectory for himself or herself and for others. As our leaders have grown, they have increasingly recognized the importance and the power of alignment, and their own alignment skills have grown accordingly. Over time, we have developed a culture full of practical alignment strategies that impact teachers and students every day.

LEADERSHIP IN ACTION

Teacher Alignment in Action

An information meeting at Rocky River Elementary School in the fall of 2013 gave one third-grade teacher an opportunity to better align her efforts with the mission. She was trailing other teachers in student performance, so, at the meeting, she discussed the situation with others and learned about their classroom practices. She then observed other teachers in action and increased her focus on small-group and individual student coaching.

She aligned herself and her students with the other classes and drove the work consistently over the following weeks. In the winter information meeting nine weeks later, she and her students had leapfrogged the other classes, and she was leading her grade level.

MGSD Practical Alignment Strategies

- Teams and individuals align their work with the digital conversion.

- Teachers align their work with content and standards by course, content area, and grade level.

- All staff align their work with student data and student outcomes on an ongoing basis.

- Teachers align student work with the mission by encouraging and acknowledging individual and collaborative effort.

- Grade-level and department meetings focus on alignment.

- Mentors coach new hires toward all aspects of alignment.

- Our annual convocation celebration, before school starts, fosters staff, student, family, and community alignment.

A few years ago, we recognized that we had to address some tough issues in order to align our program with our mission of every child, every day. We had to look at the higher rate of suspensions for African-American students, the

Teacher leader Becky Brock helping third-grade students work collaboratively at Park View Elementary School

different graduation rates of subgroups, and the need to build confidence in our community. We started with data transparency and worked to build belief in every student among our staff.

It has taken several years, but today our culture is fully aligned with a belief in all children and a shared commitment to work together, and we believe the results speak for themselves.

LEADERSHIP VOICE

Aligning the Needs of Exceptional Students with the Mission

By **Sandy Albert**
Director of Exceptional Children's Services, MGSD

In my first months as the MGSD director of exceptional children's (EC) services, I observed teachers and listened to their concerns to determine how we could best work together to increase student engagement, close achievement gaps for students with disabilities, and fulfill our mission of every child, every day. At the same time, I worked with parents to understand their needs, and I developed relationships with our principals, assistant principals, and central office staff, who supported us with several book study groups on leadership skills.

In the fall of 2012, I developed a core leadership team made up of a compliance specialist, a psychologist, a behavior specialist, and a lead EC teacher from each school. The team met monthly during the first year, with the goal of developing a shared vision among key EC teachers that could translate back to the individual school cultures. Distributing the leadership among EC staff was key to the success of this effort and to successful outcomes for students.

Using Michael Fullan's work on changing culture in *The Six Secrets of Change*, we set out to develop a collaborative culture in the EC department. The first step was to build a sense of trust among the EC staff and a commitment to teamwork, even though the EC teachers were spread out across seven schools.

We communicated with each other about what we each needed to be successful so that we could work together to meet the needs of all stakeholders, especially the students. Our monthly EC parent advisory group meetings became more collaborative, with parents helping to develop our continuous improvement performance plan (CIPP).

In 2013, we added another school psychologist and a transition specialist to help improve the referral process and the transition services for students with disabilities. We also shifted the focus toward improving academic and social outcomes.

Every EC teacher received professional development at the school and district levels, including two sessions a month run by our core leadership team. Topics included compliance indicators, the eligibility process, technology in the self-contained classroom, and using the available resources to work collaboratively with general education teachers. With agreement from our principals, we set up additional collaborative time during early release days for our self-contained teachers to meet and develop lesson plans, write IEPs, and unpack the extended content standards.

I also met with other EC directors in our region and developed a collaborative group for compliance specialists, which is now led by our MGSD compliance specialist. The group ensures that all the districts in our region are consistent with best practices and compliance standards.

In 2014, we added a preschool coordinator and also changed our meeting schedule to include more professional development sessions. I attend several of the sessions to support our core leaders, ensure that professional development is aligned with our plans, and support daily collaboration between the EC leadership team and EC teachers. I also meet monthly with principals and central office staff to work toward district- and school-level goals.

Brilliant Consistency

Our cultural alignment helps to build a phenomenon I call "brilliant consistency," which is also supported by our formal leadership-building programs. When teachers and staff are inspired to consistently align their work with our goals and mission, teaching and learning flourish.

We often think of consistency in terms of schedules and processes, but there is another kind of consistency—the consistency that comes from growing and

April Davala, instructional technology facilitator at Mooresville High School, working with Mary Kidwell, medical science teacher at N. F. Woods Advanced Technology and Arts Center

believing together—that has lifted our efforts at MGSD. Although it is not easy to develop the ability of individuals and teams to "stick with it," consistent adherence to a work routine and work ethic are at the heart of school success.

Constant attention by all leaders is needed to combat fatigue, drudgery, and bad days and create the "it's a great day to learn" vibe that drives alignment to the mission. And there is a huge payoff. Consistency is far from dull when it translates to student and staff success.

Brilliant consistency streamlines our efforts in the right direction, supports the daily discipline needed to forge new teaching and learning design elements, and makes new ideas and strategies routine through the daily work of students and staff.

I believe that consistency and quality go hand in hand, and we work to make sure our students receive consistent high-quality care and direction from their teachers. At our Summer Connection Conference, where we offer training for other districts, participants always comment on the caring and enthusiastic energy of our teachers.

VISITOR FEEDBACK   *"I didn't see one single student off task, and I was in several schools spanning hours. I talked to lots of students, and they all knew what they were doing and why they were doing it. I didn't see any magic tricks, just consistently engaged students and teachers working together and enjoying it."*

—Dr. Steve Joel
Superintendent, Lincoln Public Schools, Nebraska

Brilliant consistency extends beyond our instructional staff to our entire support team. Our maintenance and custodial teams constantly strive for improvement, and I am always proud when our visitors talk about their obvious leadership disposition and the cleanliness of our facilities.

Similarly, our central office staff of only nine people rises to every occasion and does whatever needs to be done. In addition to their extensive duties managing payroll, HR, finance, procurement, and the reception desk, team members go above and beyond to consistently align their efforts with the mission.

They help run the Mooresville Education Foundation Golf Tournament, greet and direct visitors, support the Summer Connection Conference, assist with

Assistant principal intern Alicia Davis reviewing paperwork with finance and HR assistant Torie Ammon

laptop deployment, serve meals and refreshments, help out at PTO meetings, and engage in much more—all with an attitude of relentless cheerfulness. They are a leadership force that positively impacts everyone every day.

Alignment Lessons from Henrico County

In 2002, when I worked in Henrico County, Virginia, we deployed 26,000 laptops, and I remember the ongoing struggle to maintain alignment and focus, to interweave alignment and accountability. At the time, Bill Parker, who later joined MGSD as executive director of secondary schools, was the principal of Henrico High School, the only high school in the district that was not fully accredited.

The school suffered from pockets of low expectations for students and a lack of focus. The teachers were talented, but they did not function as a team, and many behaved as if they did not believe students could learn at high levels. Student achievement results were low in several subjects and grade levels.

The goals I gave to Bill were to improve the learning climate, increase the use of instructional technology, and become fully accredited. It was clear that building collective capacity would be key to accomplishing these goals. We decided to focus on getting everyone pulling in the same direction and building a team that would work together and believe together—in other words, on aligning beliefs with actions.

Vision

Bill determined that we needed a clear vision of what we wanted Henrico High School to become because the vision and goals needed to be in place before the work of alignment could begin. It was essential to give students and staff a mental picture of what they were expected to achieve as a school family. They needed a reputation to uphold and a target to hit—a goal to align their work with.

So Bill's team posted the school goals and a picture of a pole vaulter going over the bar in every classroom. The mission was communicated at every meeting—faculty, department, leadership, student assemblies, business partnerships, and PTAs—and served to focus the decisions and actions.

Collective Capacity and Distributed Leadership

At the start, Bill knew he had to strengthen the leadership team and enlist the talents and energies of committed teacher leaders on campus. Several teachers were anxious to serve at a higher level of leadership and ready to take on greater school-wide responsibilities.

Bill looked closely at the department chairs and in some cases decided to establish co-chairs to share the responsibilities. He also expanded the number of administrative aide positions—teachers who were assigned to some administrative duties. Bill and his team examined the leadership of school committees, made some changes, and developed new committees to address building-level needs. He created an environment that escalated teacher participation and collaboration and increased productivity.

Bill knew that success would not be possible without a team approach and a collective commitment to move the school in the right direction. He knew that this was the time to generate excitement and stress the importance of cooperation. Everyone pledged to work for the greater good of the school and understood that the school reform effort depended on a shared undertaking aligned to goals.

Communication

The leadership team increased communication on campus. Effective communication was essential because the needs of the students were so great. Communication was key to building relationships, advancing school goals, and expressing to the staff that we have a moral obligation to help every student succeed.

Bill and his team wanted to make clear that alignment with the mission was the goal of all activity, regardless of students' ability, background, or family income, and that we were committed to conveying high expectations and respect for students.

Courageous Conversations and Coaching

An important part of the leadership alignment effort was an ongoing dialogue with assistant principals and staff about accountability for student learning. Organizational goals in professional growth plans played a critical role because everyone needed to understand what was expected and how they could contribute to the school's success. Everyone's job was tied to student performance.

Bill had to be willing to have some tough conversations to start the growth and alignment process. Deliberate and focused conversations created an atmosphere for professional growth and meaningful action. Authentic feedback and mini-evaluations at frequent intervals built momentum and sustained the instructional focus because everyone needed the security of knowing how he or she was performing, as well as encouragement and suggestions for improvement.

At MGSD, we use many of the same constructs that Bill used at Henrico High School to build the tight alignment that consistently connects everyone and every activity to our goal of every child, every day. Leaders constantly provide teachers, students, and staff with direction and nurturance to support the alignment we are looking for, as we follow our vision, set up opportunities for collective capacity and distributed leadership, improve communication, and engage in courageous conversations and coaching.

LEADERSHIP VOICE

The Impact of Alignment and Accountability

By **Bill Parker**

Consultant, Virginia Department of Education; Former Executive Director of Secondary Schools, MGSD; and Former Principal, Henrico High School, Virginia

At Henrico High School, we focused on alignment and accountability to improve teaching and learning and pursue our goal of full accreditation. Each department developed an improvement plan that became its road map to academic victory. The improvement plans covered the curriculum, available resources, effective assessments, collaboration, and instructional interventions—all aligned with our mission. The assistant principals provided leadership to ensure that the plans were thoughtful, inclusive, and supported by everyone in the departments.

We asked the departments to develop a laser-like focus on student achievement, with specific strategies to facilitate improvement. We expected the plans to display clarity and convey a sense of urgency and mutual accountability. Sometimes the plans were returned for further review, and this feedback led to the development of stronger blueprints for student success.

Daily classroom observations played a central role. The real work of teaching and learning took place in the classroom, so it was incumbent on the leadership team to help teachers apply effective pedagogy in the delivery of instruction. The administrative team and the department chairs increased their visibility, support, and interventions to help improve the quality of the learning experiences for students.

We knew we could succeed only through ongoing staff development, courageous conversations, and honest feedback, with the focus always on results. We had to align lesson plans with the state standards, differentiate instruction according to student needs, incorporate instructional technology, and monitor assessment results and interventions.

I'm proud to say that we achieved full accreditation after two years, and I called Dr. Edwards as soon as I heard the news. He drove over immediately and made a special announcement to the entire school community. Students, teachers, and staff ran out onto the sidewalk, yelling, cheering, and jumping up and down. It reminded me of winning a state championship, only better.

MGSD school board members are always up to speed on the data and aligned with our mission of constantly improving outcomes for all children. At a recent school board meeting, each principal gave an overview of his or her school improvement plan and spoke with conviction about strategies to guide the work of improving student achievement.

After the plans were presented, school board member Sue Wilson rose to her feet and asked the group to join her in applauding our principals for their great work. As she stood up and clapped, the rest of the school board joined her. Everyone witnessed a fine example of cultural alignment and an important nurturing of our school leaders.

REFLECTIVE QUESTIONS

1. Do you consciously align everything you do with your major goals?

2. What practical strategies foster consistent alignment with your mission?

3. In what ways does your special education staff work on alignment to the mission?

4. How do you emphasize the importance of consistency?

5. How can you help your staff consistently grow and believe together?

REFERENCES

Fullan, Michael. (2008). *The Six Secrets of Change: What the Best Leaders Do to Help Their Organizations Survive and Thrive.* San Francisco, CA: Jossey-Bass.

Fullan, Michael, & Langworthy, Maria. (2014). *A Rich Seam: How New Pedagogies Find Deep Learning.* Boston, MA: Pearson.

Chapter 4

Cultural Conditions for Shared Leadership

"Leaders united in a common culture ultimately impact student achievement."

When a teacher at Mooresville High School, Ms. Passarelli, had to take early maternity leave, no experienced or certified teachers were available to take her place. So principal Mike Royal reached out to Joe Newman, a former student who had just graduated from Vanderbilt and was waiting to start graduate school. "Joe is a natural leader," Mike told me. "He was the captain of the North Carolina state championship track and cross country teams I coached a few years ago. He's been here a couple of weeks now and is doing a great job."

When we walked into Mr. Newman's room, the students were focused on an assignment, and Mr. Newman was acting as a roving conductor of instruction, looking very much like the students in his class. I shook his hand and thanked him for stepping up to help. As we left the room, Mike mentioned that student performance on the third-quarter assessment was up, even with the young substitute. "Ms. Passarelli has been grading papers and is in regular contact with Joe, so we haven't missed a beat," he said.

When the right cultural conditions are in place, schools and districts can build leaders at every level, among teachers, students, administrators, parents, staff, and community members. And the relationship is symbiotic. Just as culture is essential to building leaders, leaders are essential to building culture—and leaders united in a common culture ultimately impact student achievement.

However, leadership is not a destination or a short run. It takes sustained effort and focus over time, and sometimes we see the sweetest results from the folks who jump on board a little late in the game. In November 2014, at a data meeting at N. F. Woods Advanced Technology and Arts Center, teacher leader and department chair Darren Bridges told us how proud he was of Tommy Chester, our construction CTE teacher. Tommy had been slow to participate in the digital conversion, but with the support of our instructional technology facilitators, he caught on and was suddenly trying new things every week. Sometimes a package that arrives late is especially precious.

Flexibility and Adaptability

Given the fast pace and constant change of our digital conversion, flexible and nimble leadership is a must at MGSD. Whether we are scrambling to find substitute teachers in an emergency or looking for new leaders to replace those who are retiring, our leadership culture has to be capable of rapid response and "out-of-the-box" thinking. Growing into our digital conversion, we have learned that flexibility and adaptability are not nice-to-haves but must-haves.

> **VISITOR FEEDBACK**   *"In our digital renaissance, modeled after the MGSD digital conversion, open-field running is a requirement. We adjust on the run, improvise as the play is going on, and expect our team to adjust as well."*
>
> —Dr. Alan Lee
> Superintendent, Baldwin County Public Schools, Alabama

It is not easy to create a culture where teachers are receptive to moving between grade levels or teams, but a flexible professional disposition is key to our staffing framework, and our principals are constantly looking for new ways to put together teacher teams to meet the needs of students. In addition, teachers have learned not to get uptight when things do not go as planned—not an easy task—and students have taught their teachers how to troubleshoot software and constantly realign activities on the run.

Many groups and departments throughout the district model flexibility and nimble leadership. The members of our maintenance department constantly respond to changing needs related to equipment, weather, and usage, and they

---

LEADERSHIP IN ACTION

Adaptability in Action

When one of our outstanding veteran principals, Robin Melton, asked to move into an assistant principal role in order to spend more time with her family, we placed her with a second-year principal, Chuck La Russo, who benefitted from working with a knowledgeable and seasoned leader.

The pair did a fantastic job at Rocky River Elementary. Our ability to be flexible had a positive impact all around, benefitting both leaders and helping the school reach new performance levels. According to Chuck, "Having Robin right beside me every day with her experience and confidence has been a constant professional boost that lifts me up all the time."

---

pride themselves on their timely response and quality work. Principals and teachers recognize them as vital team members who are respected and appreciated by all.

The eight members of our technology team, including our chief technology officer, Scott Smith, are constantly on the run, leading the maintenance of the infrastructure, hardware, and systems functionality for more than 6,000 computers and a wireless network. They offer a fluid model of adaptability to changing circumstances from which we all can learn.

Graciousness and Acknowledgement

When leaders lead with graciousness, they are kind, polite, and respectful in their interactions with others, and they treat others as they would wish to be treated themselves. I have long believed that a school culture that encourages gracious behavior among students and staff benefits in many ways.

Graciousness establishes the value of individuals, even when they may have fallen short of expectations, and it is highly effective when direction and encouragement are delivered respectfully. Graciousness is not only the right thing to do; it gets results. A little extra acknowledgement energizes the daily efforts of all.

Leaders have a responsibility to serve, and when they serve with respect and honor for others, they lead well. Our leaders have all grown in their ability to lead with graciousness, and we have evolved in our work as a mutual affirmation society. Leaders continuously thank teachers, colleagues, and students, building a culture of "leadership manners" that has permeated our schools.

First-grade teacher Beverly Stewart acknowledging a student's effort at Park View Elementary School

Although we are relentlessly enthusiastic about innovation, we understand and embrace some traditional elements of leadership development. My mother told me that manners would open doors, and she was right. A simple thank you can reap huge benefits. In my view, good leaders let people know that they care all the time. Courtesy, respect, and manners are interwoven in the social fabric of our schools, and it is essential that anyone in a leadership role demonstrate these traits.

LEADERSHIP IN ACTION

Graciousness in Action

When our leadership team read Tom Chiarella's *Esquire* article "How to Be Gracious and Why," we reflected on what the article meant for us. Lenoa Smith, the assistant principal at Park View Elementary, made the following comment: "Graciousness looks easy, but it's not. And we shouldn't mistake manners for graciousness. Manners are rules. They are helpful, yes. But graciousness reflects a state of being. If we really care about our kids, we will care about each other. We have to live graciously if we want our students to be gracious."

When we are asking teachers to evolve, align their work with the mission, and optimize student achievement, we have to recognize their progress with encouraging words and a nurturing attitude. MGSD leaders build momentum by thanking and acknowledging teachers and staff whenever they see evidence of good work.

For example, I love visiting classrooms and praising the students and teachers in front of the principal. Our principals, central office leaders, and others all follow this strategy to help build a constant vibe of "yes, we can" in order to nurture movement in the right direction.

When I visit each MGSD class a couple of times a year, unscheduled, with the principal or assistant principal, I comment on teachers' specific contributions and let them know how grateful we are to have them on the team. They generally tell me that they appreciate the acknowledgement and the attention of colleagues.

This work, which may appear mundane or perfunctory, is in fact essential and highly effective when carried out with focused energy. Thanking teachers in front of their students and calling attention to the importance of their classrooms is not a matter of secondary importance. After 20 years of serving as a superintendent, I am just beginning to understand how important acknowledgement is in moving our schools forward.

LEADERSHIP VOICE

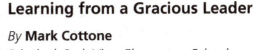

Learning from a Gracious Leader

By **Mark Cottone**
Principal, Park View Elementary School

When I was an assistant principal at Park View Elementary, with three years of experience, I was accustomed to the mundane but essential management duties such as discipline, transportation, and resource management that are needed to run a school. However, I was unfamiliar with the transformational leadership that can take a school to the next level.

Crystal Hill, the principal at that time, is responsible for unleashing my leadership potential through her gracious leadership and constant encouragement. To increase my capacity for leading others, she encouraged me to pursue a doctoral degree in educational leadership and lead several initiatives within our school.

> Dr. Hill appreciated the potential in me when I saw only what was in front of me. She let me stand with her in making almost every school decision, fostering my personal growth. As my leadership skills expanded under her influence, my goals shifted from a personal focus to a school and district focus, and I began to imagine our school reaching the highest level of student achievement.
>
> When Dr. Hill accepted a promotion, I applied for the position of principal. I was fueled by a passion to move the school to the next level, and I prepared for my interview with a 100-day plan designed to move Park View forward and become a North Carolina Honor School of Excellence. In my second year as principal, we achieved our goal.

Impact on Students

Many visitors have commented on the gracious attitude of MGSD students. I think the decorum and manners of our students reflect how they are treated by the adults in our schools. On a recent visit to East Mooresville Intermediate, I asked some fourth-grade students how their new teacher was doing. "She's doing great. She likes us, and we like her," one little girl responded. "How do you know she likes you?" I asked. "Because she tells us all the time," a boy volunteered.

MGSD students are involved with several team- and culture-building efforts that shape how we treat each other. Two programs, Capturing Kids' Hearts at Mooresville High School and Mooresville Middle School and PBIS (Positive Behavior Intervention System) at the other MGSD schools, focus on creating a respectful and caring classroom culture. Both programs help students work together to build a culture of appreciating diversity and enjoying learning in a collaborative environment. We take this work very seriously and dedicate time and resources to the effort.

> **VISITOR FEEDBACK**   *"Your students are so polite and mannerly and so willing and able to explain what they are doing."*
>
> —Dr. Kevin Singer
> Executive Director, Central Susquehanna Intermediate Unit, Pennsylvania

Impact on Work Ethic

MGSD staff respond to gracious leadership by working hard. The positive flow of communication gives everyone the energy to stick with it and get through it, elevating their productivity and well-being. We want to model dedication and hard work for our students. We work hard, and we expect them to work hard also.

VISITOR FEEDBACK   *"I've been talking to your teachers about their after-school tutoring. You have got to have the hardest-working teachers on the planet."*

—Larry Colbourne
President, Mebane Foundation

Our teachers constantly go above and beyond to meet the needs of students. Our principals are in classrooms every day, attentive to keeping the focus on the work. Our custodians are vigilant about keeping our schools clean, and our maintenance staff hustle. Our bus drivers, cafeteria staff, child nutrition staff, office staff, and all the members of the MGSD team are expected to work hard every day, and they do.

The alignment of nurturing and direction has made us all accountable for each other. As we model our work for each other and focus on learning goals, everyone hears the message that he or she counts and plays a role in our success. Everyone shares in and celebrates our success along with his or her colleagues.

LEADERSHIP IN ACTION

Dedication in Action

One August day, I was leaving the laptop deployment area and hustling back to the office for a meeting. I saw Melton Johnson, Mooresville High School head custodian, and Napoleon Lowery, Mooresville High School custodian and assistant boys' basketball coach, hauling a load of stuff from the annex over to the main campus on the dilapidated Gator. The heat was like a hot, wet blanket as I walked over to them.

Melton told me he had been worried about getting everything done the following week, when he was planning to help the new teachers move in and set up their rooms. "Then, in walks Napoleon," he told me. "And he said he was going to come in on Saturday to get everything done, so I told him I would be there with him. An hour later Kenneth and Tim told me the same thing. I didn't even have to ask. They just knew." I thanked Melton for his leadership and told him what a profound difference he and his team made for our students.

Team Spirit

One of the most important tasks of leaders charged with improving schools is building a sense of team spirit across the organization. Unfortunately, many school reform efforts have fallen short because of a lack of attention to team spirit and the human factor. The efforts often focus on the hardware and technical infrastructure. Even the professional development discussion generally does not focus on the human infrastructure, although it has a far greater impact on success.

People Power

At MGSD, as we learned to use digital resources and a new pedagogical framework, we also focused on building team spirit. Although many factors have contributed to our progress, our primary success factor has been people power from day one. That power has grown out of our distributed leadership philosophy, which has led to an increasing number of people investing energy, time, and intellect—as well as heart and soul—in our mission.

First-grade teachers Hilary Miller, from Rocky River Elementary School, and Frank Saraco, from Park View Elementary School, working together

VISITOR FEEDBACK *"Throughout our partnership with Mooresville, I have had the opportunity to hear about the MGSD vision from multiple stakeholders. The thing that has always impressed me the most is that each of these stakeholders consistently shares the same story, embodies the same passion, and shares the same vision for students."*

—Bill Goodwyn
Chief Executive Officer, Discovery Education

Because we are a team, we believe that we are all responsible for helping each other grow and be successful in our work, from every student to every teacher to every bus driver. When school districts invest in human capital, the circle of influence widens, and the push to move the organization forward gathers strength. A boat with five people pulling their oars in unison moves ahead more rapidly than a boat with 10 people rowing in different directions.

In *Leadership and the New Science*, Margaret Wheatley writes about the ideas of team spirit and "field force," and how they develop coherence throughout an organization or culture:

> "Field [spirit] creation is not just the work of senior managers. Every employee has energy to contribute. We need to be very serious about the work of field creation because fields give form to our words."

LEADERSHIP IN ACTION

Team Spirit in Action

Team spirit is always on display at our annual occupational course of study (OCS) winter presentations, when students from N. F. Woods Advanced Technology and Arts Center who have overcome many obstacles impress us with the quality of their multimedia presentations. We recognize their leadership and accomplishments.

At the OCS winter presentation in 2012, the principal of Mooresville High School, Mike Royal, congratulated three OCS students who had shown outstanding team spirit by encouraging and helping others, especially new students. All the OCS students received enthusiastic applause from their peers in the audience, who feel part of the school family, share in each other's successes, and support those who struggle.

Teamwork is integral to school innovation and to every aspect of school, student, and teacher success. A guiding team spirit that touches hearts and includes everyone in a family-like community undergirds and strengthens everything we do at MGSD. This spirit of collegial endeavor has allowed teachers to collectively work through challenges and build their capacity to lead, learn, solve problems, and share responsibility for success and accountability.

Shared Lifting

I believe that if everyone lifts, everyone is lifted. If teachers and staff work together to improve student performance in a school district, momentum kicks in, and the performance level of teachers and staff rises.

When people work collaboratively, when teachers and students develop their skills together in a digital conversion initiative, the force of that effort meets the lift from teachers and students growing and achieving success over time. Then great things can happen. We have seen it in terms of student achievement, with an academic composite and graduation rate consistently near the top in the state.

Because of our collaborative approach, it took only a few years to build our culture and productivity to a high level. We saw improvement along the way, and

LEADERSHIP IN ACTION

Shared Lifting in Action

Over the years, each member of the science department at Mooresville High School has developed his or her skills in certain content areas. Now the team looks strategically at how to maximize productivity, with a tactical plan that has teachers moving in and out of each other's classrooms to enhance instruction according to individual teaching strengths. This roving instructional strategy has achieved record-setting results.

In a recent third-quarter data meeting, Scott Bruton, the science department chair, told us that he and his team were struggling with how to help students adjust to the rigor of the new tests. "But if we keep sharing little successes with each other and using each other's skills, we'll make progress. Our collegial teamwork has never been better, and we are determined," he said.

we were quick to declare progress when and where we could, early and often. We took incremental steps, and we kept moving forward. Momentum driven by shared lifting is a beautiful thing.

LEADERSHIP VOICE

Collaboration and Shared Lifting

By **Allen Stevens**
Science Department Chair, Mooresville Middle School

My mind-set as a leader at MGSD has evolved from top-down messages to collaborative messages. If I needed to get something done in the past, I passed the information down. Now we work as a department with a shared vision of where we need to go and the tasks we need to accomplish. This collaborative model forces teachers, especially young teachers, to think more critically about how we can improve.

We talk with each other about what worked, what did not work, and what we can do to make things better. New teachers bring new ideas and techniques to the table that they may have kept to themselves in the past because they did not believe they had a voice. In the collaborative model, they have the freedom to share their ideas, while the more experienced teachers also make their contributions.

Two new young teachers in our school, Justin James and Courtney Clark, have influenced many outstanding veteran teachers and boosted some veterans to renew their commitment to innovation, collaboration, and productivity. The result has been improved academic performance and a significant improvement in "can do" attitude.

My focus has shifted from being nervous about data sharing to seeing it as a collaborative opportunity for growth. The teacher leader academy has played an important part in this change, helping us to look at data together and integrate a new approach to our work on a consistent basis.

Over the years at MGSD, we have transitioned from a department-level mind-set to a collaborative school-wide mind-set. For example, I now feel I have a responsibility to teach students to read and write more technically in science, so I am incorporating English instruction into science and partnering with the English department in this effort.

Encouragement and Mentoring

In the early stages of MGSD's digital conversion initiative, everyone needed a lot of encouragement. Learning how to teach in a new way, use digital resources, and embrace the transparent use of data were monumental changes for the entire district. So at every meeting, in addition to troubleshooting, we spent time talking up the good stuff. We discussed student projects that blew us away and the upward tilt in our achievement results that convinced us we were on the right track.

Understanding the new learning management system was challenging for some teachers, but we kept them going with a constant message of support that said, "You can do it, and together we'll make it happen." Every day, colleagues and friends offered to help and mentor each other, greatly increasing our ability to build capacity, culture, and leadership.

At faculty meetings, principals' meetings, school board meetings, and staff picnics, we celebrated the small victories of teachers, students, and staff, encouraging them to keep up the good work with sustained directional nurturance.

Today, our principals and assistant principals are in and out of classrooms all day long, encouraging students and teachers and offering direction and nurturance. When I asked South Elementary third-grade teacher Scott Roper how he was doing after his first year at MGSD, he replied, "The folks here—my principal, the child nutrition staff, the custodians, and all the third-grade team—are always reaching out to me to offer assistance and encouragement. It's like having a bunch of mothers watching over me!"

Our formal mentoring program, the Beginning Teacher Support Program, supports new hires from day one. Mentors help new teachers with everything from finding their way around the building to getting reports done on time to managing difficult situations. We provide training and workshops for our mentors to enhance their quality and consistency.

Our formal student mentoring program, Change a Life, pairs up students at all grade levels with adult mentors. We provide training for mentors, along with guidelines and ideas about how to build relationships with students and positively influence their lives inside and outside school.

Each year at our Change a Life celebration, the mentors and mentees gather to celebrate their work together. I always enjoy seeing the Mooresville chief of police, Carl Robbins, at our high school football games with his mentee. Many other community members have joined in this effort and provided external leadership for our students.

Mentoring in Action

In the early days of our digital conversion, we needed to try out the initiative on a small scale before rolling it out district-wide. Under the leadership of the Mooresville High School English department chair, Nancy Gardner, the English department volunteered to be the guinea pigs, with carts in every English class during the first year and laptops for every student from the second year on.

The level of technology expertise varied widely. The younger teachers took a leadership role and mentored the veteran teachers, which quickly led to an atmosphere of support, gratitude, and trust. The role reversal had a serendipitous effect. The two groups began to collaborate more. They encouraged each other in the new work and shared ideas, tools, lesson plans, and assessments.

In the words of Nancy Gardner, "Those of us who were old timers were not as comfortable with computers, but the younger teachers figured things out on their own and taught us. We benefitted from differentiated instruction from our young mentors, with extended time and support for those of us who needed it."

In *A Rich Seam: How New Pedagogies Find Deep Learning*, Michael Fullan and Maria Langworthy describe the conditions and the leadership needed to support new pedagogy such as a digital conversion. They believe that culture and capacity building must be supported by encouragement and affirmation, a belief that we at MGSD share.

Seeing the potential in others and mentoring them to achieve that potential are important leadership tasks. When we build the capacity of others, we also build our own. At MGSD we go out of our way to encourage our colleagues to move up to the next level of responsibility. For example, our principals constantly talk to their assistant principals about when they will be principals and encourage them to view their work as opportunities to evolve as leaders.

When I worked with three MGSD leaders on the plans for a massive renovation project at Mooresville High School, I encouraged them to use the experience as an opportunity to prepare to become superintendents. Over the years, I have had the good fortune to work with a host of extraordinary leaders and have encouraged many of them to become superintendents, including the following, many of whom have pursued their own digital conversions:

- Rosa Atkins, Charlottesville, Virginia
- Tom Baily, Oak Ridge, Tennessee (retired)
- Bobby Browder, Prince George's County, Virginia
- Luvelle Brown, Ithaca, New York
- Dallas Dance, Baltimore County, Maryland
- Bill Hite, Philadelphia, Pennsylvania
- Tony Jackson, Nash-Rocky Mount, Virginia
- Eric Jones, Powhatan County, Virginia
- Pat Kinlaw, Henrico County, Virginia
- David Myers, New Kent County, Virginia
- Katrise Perera, Isle of Wight County, Virginia

Crystal Hill, executive director of elementary schools, working with Mark Cottone, principal of Park View Elementary School

- Ed Pruden, Brunswick County, North Carolina
- Aaron Spence, Virginia Beach, Virginia

In our nation's schools today, we face so many challenges that teachers and staff need constant words of encouragement as well as positive expectations from their leaders in order to align their work with their goals every day. A nurturing culture provides the foundation to give both positive and tough feedback, as well as structured directions, because it allows all parties to recognize that aligning activities toward a common goal is the number-one priority.

Leadership Voice

Encouraging Leadership in Others

By **Crystal Hill**
Executive Director of Elementary Schools, MGSD

While shared leadership has always been an essential element in my leadership style, my leadership improved when I returned to Mooresville from another district. The level of expectation was at an all-time high, and, while I was effective, I had to step up to the new challenges.

As a leader, I have the responsibility to encourage others to discover that they have talents and mentor them to reach their potential. Building the leadership capacity of stakeholders fuels our collective work. The vision and heart of the work we love take off because we are empowering colleagues to lead and effect change.

A shared leadership model and an across-the-board commitment to excellence allowed me to tap into the talents of others to fill my own deficits or inexperience in certain areas. This model is essential for me as a leader and those I work with. Others see my openness to diverse ideas and styles while I support them in their growth.

Creativity and Innovation

Leaders who cultivate creativity and innovation, as opposed to routine and rigidity, prosper in the fluid MGSD culture. Our teachers and students are constantly finding new online content, investigating the dynamic digital world, and connecting

Creativity in Action

When a group of visitors walked into Mr. Fulton's English class at Mooresville Middle School, they saw students working on team projects all over the place. One group was sitting on the floor, and another was working in the hallway. Students were walking around the room talking to each other, and the air buzzed with activity and communication.

Seeing that some visitors were unsure what to make of the situation, Mr. Fulton commented, "Yes, it's kind of organized chaos in here. But everyone's working, and they have deadlines. It took us a couple of years to really get this down, but we adjusted to it, and now we're all comfortable with the new culture."

One of the guests later told me that she had to switch to more creative thinking to recognize that these students were being productive in a nontraditional classroom environment.

with it to improve teaching and learning. Leaders are always looking for new ways to engage students while supporting independence, interdependence, and individual and team discipline. Trying new stuff keeps us fresh.

As teachers and students have learned to solve problems, they have allowed for and authorized creativity. It took some time for many of our staff to trust that students will do what they need to do and figure out how they need to do it, but now a high level of authorized creativity allows students to be more successful in countless ways—from developing movies that match the content they are being taught to building research projects that require collaboration and discipline over time.

We are in the process of formalizing new instructional strategies that further promote creativity and productivity as well as incorporate the resources of our digital conversion and our project-based and inquiry-based methodology. Starting in the fall of 2014, we implemented "gateway projects," whereby third, sixth, eighth, and 12th-grade students build a long-term multimedia research project and present it to a panel of judges.

This type of work aligns with the work students will be asked to do in their future lives. Malcolm Gladwell suggests in his book *Outliers: The Story of Success* that the ability to create something over an extended period of time is one of the most important indicators of personal success.

Language and Conversation

Language counts, and I believe that what we hear shapes who we are. When I was in school, my mother called out to me and my brother every morning, "Wake up, it's another great day!"—words that had a profound impact on me. And although my daughters always groaned when I called up to them in the morning, "It's a great day to learn," I believe they heard the message. What we say to each other matters, and how we say it matters.

Language is especially important in a distributed leadership model. At MGSD, we do not wait for answers to come from someone or somewhere else. Rather, we build leadership capacity through language and conversation, authorizing leaders all over the place to talk about their work, their learning, and their experiences, to help scaffold our trajectory.

We always have many conversations going on. Students are constantly collaborating in teams, and their conversations give them a new level of engagement and a new ability to apply what they are learning. Teachers and other staff are always talking to each other, formally and informally.

Teachers highly value the time that is formally dedicated to working on strategies, data, challenges, and problem solving. But they also benefit from the ongoing informal teacher–principal conversations, however brief, that are incredibly important in moving them forward. All our leaders offer these "collegial whispers" to others, constantly encouraging the work of collaboration and high academic achievement.

The word "work" is very important at MGSD. In our classrooms, hallways, and media centers, students discuss their "work" with each other, a subtle but huge change in the way students talk about assignments and homework. Teachers and other school leaders also have a running conversation about their "work," a conversation that ranges from academic objectives to socializing and organizing. This professional, collegial dialogue is central to our instructional methodology and shared achievement.

Teachers, students, principals, and others at MGSD constantly talk about what we are trying to do and the best way to do it—a language of learning that includes the voices of new leaders in classrooms all over the district. We use the language of teamwork and shared responsibility in all our departmental, grade-level, faculty, and principals' meetings, listening to the contributions of our leaders while encouraging discussion and participation. This fosters a kind of conversation I call "reflective dialogue," which leads in turn to "reflective advancement."

Trust and Conviction

Trusting someone is a big deal, and telling individuals or teams that you trust them sends a powerful message. When school leaders develop relationships with teachers and staff, an organic sense of mutual trust needs to evolve.

I have always loved Antoine de Saint-Exupéry's *The Little Prince*, a fanciful tale about a prince who learns from others in order to teach us. The author emphasizes how long it takes for trust to develop between people and how trust, once broken, can rarely be repaired.

Building trust does indeed take time and usually grows out of shared challenges that are overcome together. I was able to build trust with our principals out of a shared conviction that we could overcome the challenges and work together to help our students succeed. That conviction, which is also shared by our teachers, is amplified by the trust we have in each other. But there are no shortcuts to building trust and conviction. It takes time and commitment.

As part of the trust we have built, we at MGSD share the same convictions around achieving our goals:

Shared Convictions

- *Every child* means *every child*—no exceptions.
- Confidence in every child takes work and does not come easily.
- Working at working together, however difficult, translates into progress for children.
- Everyone needs to demonstrate a voracious appetite for learning.
- Working through disagreements and turbulence is essential for the good of the students.
- Every day is unlike any other day, and we must live up to the opportunity.

Sympathy and Love

During my career as a superintendent, I have seen the power of sympathy, empathy, and love lift individuals and organizations many times. When someone you love and respect loses someone he or she loves and respects, a natural caring should follow in organizations, just as it does among close friends and family members. Leaders must model sympathy, empathy, and love so that these values become widespread throughout the organization.

I have seen colleagues who have suffered loss or tragedy helped and sometimes healed by the caring of others. I often hear our students and parents say, "We love our teacher," and our team members tell each other, "We love you." When schools, faculties, and school systems work at building a sense of institutional caring and love for each other, they are working on one of the most powerful aspects of leadership and culture.

It was dripping hot when we assembled in the Mooresville Middle School gym on June 6, 2013, but most of us were oblivious to the heat. President Barack Obama was due on stage in less than 30 minutes, and the energy and excitement were palpable.

Less than a week before, a staff person at the U.S. Department of Education had called to let me know that a special guest would be visiting. At first I was sure that the vague wording pointed to Secretary of Education Arne Duncan. We later heard that Secretary Duncan would indeed be visiting—along with the president of the United States. President Obama had chosen to come to our district to announce the plan to extend wireless connectivity to all classrooms in the United States with a realignment of E-Rate funding. Many MGSD leaders worked with the White House staff to plan and execute the visit.

When we heard the thudding of the Marine One helicopters overhead, the gym erupted in cheers and applause. Mooresville is a politically conservative community, but the recognition of our work transcended politics, and everyone there was part of a proud and collaborative dynamic. We knew we were sharing something that would stay with each of us forever and that the recognition was not about individuals but about our team.

Our team spirit, developed through the dedicated work of hundreds of leaders at all levels, had brought us to this day, lifted us during hard times, and powered us to work with sustained vigor. After the president spoke in the gym, he met with a small group of teachers who were discussing the details of our digital conversion with the secretary of education. The president listened intently and said, "I love the culture here. It is inspiring."

REFLECTIVE QUESTIONS

1. How do you foster flexibility and creativity in your leaders?

2. Does your staff model a gracious attitude that students can learn from?

3. What mechanisms can you use to improve team spirit in your school or district?

4. How can you bring more love and sympathy into daily school life?

5. What shared convictions underlie your work with students?

REFERENCES

Chiarella, Tom. (May 2013). "How to Be Gracious and Why," *Esquire*.

De Pree, Max. (1990). *Leadership Is an Art*. New York, NY: Dell.

de Saint-Exupéry, Antoine. (1995). *The Little Prince*. Translated by Richard Howard. Ware, UK: Wordsworth Editions Limited.

Fullan, Michael, & Langworthy, Maria. (2014). *A Rich Seam: How New Pedagogies Find Deep Learning*. Boston, MA: Pearson.

Gladwell, Malcolm. (2008). *Outliers: The Story of Success*. New York, NY: Little, Brown and Company.

Wheatley, Margaret. (2006). *Leadership and the New Science: Discovering Order in a Chaotic World*. San Francisco, CA: Berrett-Koehler.

Chapter 5

Everyday Pathways to Leadership

"Teaching is leading, leading is teaching, and strong teachers lead every day as they go about their work."

When I was in second grade at Pleasant Ridge Elementary in Knoxville, Tennessee, Mrs. Williams coached us for several weeks in preparation for our annual Christmas program. Along with two other students, I had to memorize verses from Luke 2 and open the program with our assignment. My partners were smart girls, and I probably relied on them a little too much in our practice sessions.

When I walked into the gym with my parents on the big night, every seat was taken, and people were standing in the aisles. I saw Mrs. Williams beckoning me to come backstage. "Mark, Ruth's mom called, and she's sick, and Mary can't make it either," she whispered as we stood beside Mrs. Easterly, the principal. "I don't think I can do it without them," I said anxiously.

Mrs. Williams knelt down and looked me in the eye. "Mark, you can do this," she said. Mrs. Easterly got ready to open the curtain. "Mark, we're counting on you," she said. Somehow I managed to make it through, and over the years, I have reflected many times on this experience. Today I believe it was the first time I was offered a leadership pathway.

Teaching is leading, leading is teaching, and strong teachers lead every day as they go about their work. In addition to our formal programs of leadership growth, we consistently foster leadership across all stakeholder groups.

We integrated the intentional design of leadership capacity building into our work at MGSD from the beginning of our digital conversion initiative. Margaret Wheatley's concept of the force field has been a component of this effort and has had a huge impact on our work for several years. According to Wheatley in *Leadership and the New Science*, the force field must reach all corners of the organization, involve everyone, and be available everywhere:

> "Vision statements move off the walls and into the corridors, seeking out every employee, every recess in the organization. In the past, we may have thought of ourselves as skilled designers of organizations, assembling the pieces, drawing the boxes, exerting energy to painstakingly create all the necessary links, motivation, and structures. Now we need to imagine ourselves as beacon towers of information, standing tall in the integrity of what we say, pulsing out congruent messages everywhere. We need all of us out there, stating, clarifying, reflecting, modeling, filling all of space with the messages we care about. If we do that, a powerful field develops—and with it, the wondrous capacity to organize into coherent, capable form."

I believe that a positive cultural force field can be felt and seen in all MGSD schools, largely as a result of the ubiquitous leadership of our teachers and teachers valuing the shared culture of which they are a part.

New teachers feel the uplift of high expectations, wrapped up in coaching, encouragement, and respect from other staff. Veteran staff are challenged to grow, with a constant pulse of encouragement coming from students, parents, and teachers. Support staff are highly valued. And students working in our team culture emulate our leadership force field and take it with them into the classroom.

VISITOR FEEDBACK   *"Now more than ever, we need new constructs for thinking about the type of leadership necessary in our public schools. We serve in a rapidly changing, highly complex, and politically charged milieu that demands accountability and empowerment at all levels of the organization.*

How can we have coherency from a whole systems perspective while creating autonomy to act with focus, based on the unique needs of our schools, staff, and students? Distributed leadership is our adaptive challenge."

—Dr. Steve Webb
Superintendent, Vancouver Public Schools, Vancouver, Washington, and member of the League of Innovative Schools

Informal Leadership Pathways for Teachers

In a traditional school leadership model, teachers are generally limited to perfunctory assignments with rules-based limits, and they have no opportunity to actually lead a school, manage an evolving pedagogical design, or balance a demanding accountability system. But I believe that today's work of accountability is so complex and dynamic that it only makes sense to have many colleagues lifting and leading.

MGSD Teacher Leadership Roles

- Department and grade-level chairs
- Digital curriculum committee members
- Teacher and principal selection committee members
- Teacher advisory committee members
- Calendar advisory committee members
- Summer Institute staff
- Summer Connection staff
- Trainers of other districts
- Coaches, music directors, and sponsors of student organizations

Our teachers grow by working together on a constantly evolving pedagogical framework in a student-centered, constructivist, and project-based classroom culture, with veteran and rookie teachers learning from each other.

As our teachers guide and influence our work, they learn and add value in numerous ways. Their reflective leadership practice helps us select online content, interview colleagues, analyze data, develop calendars, and build detailed

Teacher Growth in Action

Six years ago, we were battling the inertia of some teachers who resisted the changing pedagogical shift of the digital conversion and new efficacy demands. Some took longer than others to get on board, and we recognized that the rate of growth would vary.

Carrie Tulbert, the principal of Mooresville Middle School, sent me the following note about one such teacher, Mr. Patterson, who started out at a slow rate of growth but gradually improved over time:

"Mr. Patterson doesn't do change very well, but never out of an attitude of insubordination. Although he may not be up to the level of many others, he is improving. I believe his growth can be attributed to his willingness to seek out help from others and to the support of his team. He is also learning how to integrate technology with choices, capture kids' hearts, and use open-ended questions. I told Mr. Patterson today that I really enjoyed his class. Here are the highlights I observed:

- Mr. Patterson offered his students choices in how they presented their learning about the joint and skeletal system. And he went on to discuss with them the pros and cons of using different pieces of software for those choices.
- During class, he moved around to different pairs of students working on their projects and interacted with them in a very natural and relaxed manner.
- One group of young men was off task, and instead of using his 'big' voice, Mr. Patterson quietly said, 'I like looking at those projects, too, and they're pretty cool, but is this what you're supposed to be doing right now?'
- And then my favorite part was at the end. He asked all the students to return to their seats, and he said, 'Tell me some fun things you learned today. Any cool websites? Any cool tools?' And the kids began actively sharing!"

improvement plans, supported by the vibrancy that arises from collective, action-based experience.

Our constant study of data often provides opportunities for new leaders to pop up. New teachers may focus on a particular area that everyone wants to know about or share an insight that grade-level or department chairs want to use. As a result, new leaders and new pathways emerge constantly.

Daily Leadership Opportunities for Teachers

- Reviewing and selecting new online content
- Monitoring content and processes for effectiveness and alignment to standards
- Troubleshooting content and assessment engines for and with students
- Sharing feedback with colleagues and service providers
- Using data to identify insights into student learning
- Mentoring new teachers

These leadership opportunities have grown our staff as individuals and as teams. Consequently, I estimate that well over half of our teachers now provide significant leadership, with huge value to our students and a deep impact on our district culture. We call on and count on our teachers to provide leadership for departments and grade levels across all aspects of the work. We also celebrate new

Fifth-grade teacher leader Amy Smith, speaking to the board of education about a 2014 summer enrichment program she was leading

hires and welcome them as family members while at the same time immediately engaging them with the knowledge work of leading the digital conversion.

Our teachers have developed a powerful blend of content knowledge and digital resources and lead most of the MGSD training sessions. More and more of them are also asked to lead staff development in other districts, including Houston ISD and districts in Alabama, Missouri, Georgia, Tennessee, and South Carolina that are following or adapting the MGSD model, greatly enhancing our teachers' opportunities for personal leadership development.

In *A New Culture of Learning*, Douglas Thomas and John Brown discuss the idea that learning grows exponentially in a culture that works as a collective, a concept that we have seen borne out in our daily work:

> "As the name implies, [a collective] is a collection of people, skills, and talent that produces a result greater than the sum of its parts. For our purposes, collectives are not solely defined by shared intention, action or purpose. Rather they are defined by an active engagement with the process of learning. Communities derive their strength from creating a sense of belonging, while collectives derive theirs from participation."

LEADERSHIP VOICE

From Avoidance to Leadership

By **Tracey Waid**
*Instructional Technology Facilitator,
Mooresville High School*

When our digital conversion began, I tried really hard to avoid being a leader. I wasn't looking for "more work," which is what I associated with leadership at the time. I had just returned from maternity leave to teach a content area that was new to me, and I had two children under three and a husband who traveled regularly for work.

But six weeks later, I was enrolled in a master's program that combined literacy and technology to improve student performance. I was excited about the potential for change but also frustrated that my department did not seem to be buying in. As the youngest and only lateral-entry member of the department, I did not have the confidence to speak up.

So I quietly worked on changing my own corner of the world. I advocated for my world language department to throw out its textbook-driven, outdated curriculum and focus on thematic units with technology-infused project-based learning and authentic proficiency assessment. Despite resistance from some teachers, our school leadership encouraged me to keep pressing, and I found like-minded colleagues.

At the end of the year, I was asked to step up as department chair. Despite my desire to fly under the radar, the changes I was making had been noticed. I was wary of taking on this role since I had not been through traditional teacher education, had no official leadership experience, and was not sure how the rest of my department would react. But my principal, Mr. Royal, told me that if I did what's best for kids and kept that at the forefront, I could not go wrong.

With his support and that advice in mind, I implemented the changes I knew were needed. I established digital student portfolios to show growth and a blogging program to connect our foreign language students to the outside world, bringing the emphasis on data from the core areas into our elective area to personalize instruction. Staffing changes also brought in fresh ideas.

At our district leadership academy, I learned how to handle conflict within departments and how to grow leadership capacity in our school. I served on our school's leadership team and learned a tremendous amount from Mr. Royal. I watched him lead with action—not just words—and advocate for his staff and students, while offering opportunities for growth and establishing a culture of hard work, trust, attention to detail, and forward motion.

After three years as department chair and being recognized as my school's Teacher of the Year in 2012, I applied for the vacant instructional technology facilitator position at the high school in 2013. I was reluctant to leave my department, but I knew that in the new position, I could influence 1,800 students instead of 180. The opportunity to work with other teachers and students who might never come through my French classroom was powerful.

My district had invested in me, taught me how to be a teacher leader despite my initial resistance, and prepared me to take this next step. One year in, I'm beyond satisfied with my decision, and I enjoy working with our district's many exemplary leaders, growing students and staff as we serve as a lighthouse district for others.

Informal Leadership Opportunities for Principals and Assistant Principals

I always tell our assistant principals that one of their major jobs is to get ready to be principals, and our principals are expected to help develop their assistant principals to step into a principal role. Our assistant principals take on specific instructional leadership goals either by content area or by grade level, and we hold them accountable for the results. Similarly, many of our principals are preparing to become directors or superintendents.

This future-ready disposition has served us well. Five of our principals were promoted after serving as assistant principals, where they benefitted from multiple leadership opportunities that turbocharged their readiness. Two of our former principals have moved into assistant superintendent positions in other districts, one assistant principal is a director in another district, and a middle school assistant principal is a high school principal in another district.

Leadership opportunities for assistant principals and principals at MGSD go way beyond traditional work assignments. At most principals' meetings, we ask everyone

LEADERSHIP IN ACTION

Leadership Pathways in Action

When Mike Royal was a first-year assistant principal at Mooresville High School early in our digital conversion initiative, he was thrust into the job of leading the laptop collection process. Mike is a numbers guy, and he is big on efficiency. He broke down the process, looking for little efficiencies and saving minutes here and there.

According to Mike, "I discussed the areas of need with the staff and used my math department chair and track coaching experience to refine the procedures. Now we have it down to a science, to the point where we can retrieve over 1,800 laptops, catalog them, and store them in about an hour with no teacher stress whatsoever."

Each year Mike and his team review the process and look to make a few tweaks, mirroring the approach we take throughout our work, in which reflective practice moves us forward. The early leadership experience served Mike well in his current role as principal and offered a role model for other schools.

Cheryl Dortch, assistant principal at South Elementary School, reviewing a data wall and interactive whiteboard display with first-grade teachers

to weigh in on different topics and articulate their thoughts because opportunities to "stand and deliver" are a vital part of the development of leaders in our district.

As we work through the bumps and challenges, we make sure that school leaders are conversant with the issues and can effectively communicate with different stakeholder groups. This was an essential part of the process in the early days of our digital conversion, and it remains so.

LEADERSHIP VOICE

Broadening the Vision

By **Mike Royal**
Principal, Mooresville High School

Over the past five years, I have grown tremendously as a leader. In 2008, when we embarked on our digital conversion, I was in my second year as an assistant principal at Mooresville High School, after serving as a teacher in the school for seven years. I learned and grew under the leadership of my principal, Todd Wirt.

> I have always been a details person, but under Mr. Wirt's leadership, I was able to broaden my vision and start to see where the details fit into the larger scheme of things. This was thanks to the numerous leadership opportunities I was given in the course of the digital conversion initiative, including the opportunity to serve as the school-wide testing coordinator.
>
> I also broadened my vision through my relationships with my fellow assistant principals, who taught me about curriculum and facilities planning and how to handle tough conversations with staff members. I feel blessed to have learned from such a tremendous team during my first few years as a school administrator.

Principals and assistant principals must develop the capacity to handle tough conversations by giving feedback, constructive advice, and directive nurturance—tasks that do not come easy to many leaders. We ask our principals and assistant principals to consider the following guidelines as they develop their skills:

Handling Tough Conversations

- Talk about it now—the sooner the better.
- Honor staff by letting them know you care.
- Connect personal growth with the goals and mission.
- Point out strengths.
- Acknowledge that change is hard and takes time.
- Loop back to check on progress with immediate encouragement.
- Make sure everyone knows that growth is not optional.

Looking for Leaders in New Hires

Our hiring teams look for leadership qualities during the interview process, and our newly hired colleagues who have never worked in an environment like MGSD tell us that they treasure the new experience. Many of them respond so well to our culture that they quickly move into leadership positions themselves. Over the years, we have aligned our hiring criteria with the digital conversion and our need for teacher leaders. When we interview, we look for leadership potential in prospective candidates:

Leadership Qualities in New Hires

- Collaborative
- Collegially minded
- Effective
- Enthusiastic
- Growth-oriented
- Ready to sweat

Parents and community members also join the interview teams when we hire principals and central office leaders, extending the leadership responsibilities beyond our staff. The participatory process provides a leadership experience and allows the team to "own" the decision, ready to support new hires and make sure they are successful.

On a visit to South Elementary School in October 2013, I saw Jenifer Brown, a new special education teacher, waiting in a breakout room for her students, and I asked her how she was doing. "I feel so lucky to be in a place that cares for kids and for adults," she replied. "My mentor, Michelle Voos, has been incredibly supportive, and she checks to see how I am doing, but she really just treats me like family." Our formal mentoring program ensures that new hires feel a real sense of collegial support.

LEADERSHIP VOICE

Instant Leadership

By **Jason Gardner**
Principal, East Mooresville Intermediate School

We use a team approach in our school to hire colleagues who share our collaborative style and work ethic. That means our new hires have an instant impact, and many of them quickly move into leadership roles. Because they have different skills, they can lead across a wide range of areas:

- Caley Chase, hired as a fifth-grade English teacher in 2011, is a technology leader and the leader of our reading foundations program.
- Kourtney Clark, hired as a fourth-grade teacher in 2012, is a leader in the digital conversion and in mentoring new teachers.
- Matt Harriger, hired as a sixth-grade math teacher in 2012, is a natural leader who takes on any task and led the effort to work with one of our vendors on the re-launch of its product.
- Wendy Lewis, hired as a sixth-grade math teacher in 2012, is working toward her master's in mathematics and has become our go-to person in regard to Common Core instruction.
- Lindsay Ford, hired as a fifth-grade math teacher in 2012, has a track record of high student improvement and leads all of us in demonstrating the value of relationships with students.
- Amber Bryant, hired as a fifth-grade science teacher in 2013, quickly became the science chair for fifth grade.
- Catherine Furlong, hired as a fourth-grade English teacher in 2013, leads with her understanding of the foundations of reading instruction, the data analysis process, and personalized learning.
- Justin James, hired as a sixth-grade math teacher in 2013, shows us how to successfully facilitate learning in a collaborative classroom where kids work in groups while he steps back.

VISITOR FEEDBACK   *"MGSD principals know their teachers. They demonstrate leadership in the hiring process, ensuring an inclusive, diverse environment—all the while demanding excellence. They know what is going on in the classroom, and the evaluative process represents an opportunity for people to grow. They paint a common, clear vision for people to follow, knowing it is only through the collective efforts of all that goals will be met. They create an environment, a culture, where people are not threatened to speak up. Everyone knows that the schoolhouse (and the kids in it) are better served by an open, inclusive atmosphere of continuous improvement. This is what I felt on visiting your district."*

—John Tate
North Carolina State Board of Education Member

Most experts in different fields consider leadership development a prerequisite for organizational success. However, I think the real heart of this work resides not in formal programs or assignments but in the daily disposition of leaders to want to develop leadership in other team members. I work in a culture where leadership is modeled for others on an ongoing basis, so everyone has the opportunity to learn, and I view it as an honor to have the opportunity to develop other leaders.

When principal Chuck LaRusso and I entered Ms. Reid's first-grade class at Rocky River Elementary, a little boy waved his hand and smiled broadly at Dr. LaRusso. "Ms. Reid said she's proud of how hard I've been working," he told us. "Well, I'm proud of you, too," said Chuck.

"Ms. Reid has been working hard, too," replied the boy. We chuckled at his spontaneous leadership and encouragement of Ms. Reid.

REFLECTIVE QUESTIONS

1. How can you better integrate leadership capacity building into your school planning?
2. How do your principals model the importance of learning?
3. In what ways do you involve teachers in managing pedagogy and accountability?
4. How does your approach to leadership influence your hiring policies?
5. How do you use your regular meetings as opportunities to develop leadership?

REFERENCES

Thomas, Doug, & Brown, John S. (2011). *A New Culture of Learning: Cultivating the Imagination for a World of Constant Change.* Lexington, KY: CreateSpace.

Wheatley, Margaret. (2006). *Leadership and the New Science: Discovering Order in a Chaotic World.* San Francisco, CA: Berrett-Koehler.

Chapter 6

Formal Programs of Leadership Growth

"Leadership development must be a formal goal and an informal goal, to highlight its importance to all and to achieve the best results."

One Saturday afternoon in November 2009, I participated in a lively discussion with ten MGSD leaders and four leaders from our sister district, the Iredell-Statesville School System. This group, the Mooresville Wingate University doctoral cohort, had gathered to talk about our Skype meetings over the past five weeks with different superintendents around the country—friends and former colleagues of mine.

The energy level in the room was extremely high, although the meeting had been going since 8:30 a.m., and everyone had a full-time job as an administrator or teacher leader. I was teaching the class, called "The School Superintendent and Leadership," and even though I was flat-out tired, I was absolutely caught up in the discussion.

The opportunity to connect with several superintendents via Skype and learn about their different philosophies and experiences had made a great impression on every member of the class. The excited and insightful comments revealed the impact on the class members' own leadership paths. Every member of the cohort went on to graduate from the doctoral program, with the exception of one person who relocated in the first year.

Doctoral and Master's Cohorts

MGSD's doctoral cohorts focus on leadership, and our master's cohorts focus on school administration. Both groups have partnered with Wingate University, a small, well-regarded liberal arts college just outside Charlotte. The classes take place on our campuses during the year, which is convenient for our staff. The full summer-long program takes place on the Wingate University campus. In addition, we work with Appalachian State University to offer a blended course of study for a master's in instructional technology.

All employees receive $1,000 a year for tuition reimbursement, sometimes augmented by MGSD Foundation funding. Even when we lost ten percent of our funding and had to make painful cuts, we did not back off on our commitment to leadership and professional development. We were able to maintain our tuition reimbursement program, which sent a message that we all need to keep growing and working through the challenges.

All three graduate programs align with the need to build our leadership capacity and increase our instructional focus on digital resources. The participants boosted our efforts in the early days of our digital conversion, with the synergy of 30 or more leaders growing their individual and collective leadership capacity, and they continue to do so today, along with new cohort participants.

LEADERSHIP VOICE

Preparation for New Challenges

By **Todd Wirt**

Assistant Superintendent for Academics, Wake County Public Schools, Raleigh, North Carolina, and Former Principal, Mooresville High School

When I was the principal of Mooresville High School, I was part of a doctoral cohort at Wingate University spearheaded by Dr. Edwards. The program was provided in a convenient format that allowed me to collaborate with colleagues while prioritizing my job as principal. The instructors were current practitioners, which offered a high degree of practicality and a realistic lens into the work of executive-level leadership.

I was most influenced by two courses. The first was a course on cultural proficiency, taught by the head of the program, Dr. Lloyd Wimberly. The texts and lessons learned in this course are a part of my daily work today, where I focus on building a strong school culture across a wide range of communities. The second was the superintendency course taught by Dr. Edwards. He gave us the opportunity to Skype with superintendents and other leaders from all over the country, providing a diverse look into the work of superintendents. This course solidified my desire to one day become a superintendent myself.

Today I serve as the assistant superintendent for academics for the largest school system in North Carolina and the 15th-largest in the United States. The leadership development I received through the MGSD doctoral cohort prepared me for the challenges I face every day in a growing and highly diverse school system.

I now look for opportunities to develop leadership in others, both administrators and teachers. For example, I am leading an initiative that invests in the leadership potential of 680 teachers, in an effort to scale professional development, build capacity for shared leadership, and develop succession plans.

In addition to our doctoral and master's programs, many staff members take individual courses at local universities, and some have elected to pursue different degrees. The reflective practice and future orientation of these graduate students in our midst have driven the engine of learning in our culture. The variety of leadership growth opportunities fosters a spirit of lifelong learning and cultivates the personal and professional responsibility to learn and grow.

I check in regularly with employees who are taking classes to see how they are doing, what they are learning, and how we can support them in the difficult challenge of working full time while working through a rigorous graduate program. We acknowledge the need to balance family, work, and study, and we provide encouragement, hand holding, and nurturance to our staff.

Structure

MGSD started its doctoral and master's programs with Wingate University in the fall of 2008, after I had met with the dean of the college of education, the vice president, and the president to iron out the details. We started the master's cohort with Appalachian State University in the winter of 2009. The master's programs are two-year programs, and the doctoral program takes three to four years, so all require a high degree of commitment and sustained diligence.

We decided that applications would be approved by MGSD and the two universities, and we established two primary goals—developing a team of leaders to propel the district forward with an emphasis on student achievement and expanding our leadership capacity in the years to come.

We worked with several professors at both universities to align our evolving classroom practice with course design and focus on collaboration and hands-on projects, to make sure that our digital conversion was interwoven throughout class projects and discussions.

The master's program in instructional technology at Appalachian State University was aligned with the digital conversion in several ways. It was offered in a blended format, online and face-to-face, which enhanced our staff's understanding of how instruction is delivered and received in the digital world. It produced a cadre of teacher leaders who emerged as technology facilitators and grade-level and department leaders.

Mooresville Middle School principal Dr. Carrie Tulbert with her son after her graduation from the doctoral program, May 2012

We support both cohorts in various ways. For example, we provide coffee, water, and snacks at all classes as a small but important acknowledgement of our graduate students' efforts, and we encourage and recognize them whenever possible.

Out of the first cohorts, 26 out of 27 students completed their graduate programs and earned their degrees. Ten earned doctoral degrees, ten earned master's degrees in administration, and six earned master's degrees in instructional technology. We launched a new doctoral cohort in 2012 and a new master's cohort in 2014.

Second MGSD Doctoral Cohort, 2012

- Sandy Albert, director of exceptional children's services
- Felicia Bustle, principal, Mooresville Intermediate School
- Eisa Cox, director of secondary education, Rowan County Schools, and former assistant principal, Mooresville High School
- Angelo DelliSanti, principal, Carson High School, Rowan County Schools, and former assistant principal, Mooresville Middle School
- Chris Gammon, assistant principal, Mooresville Intermediate School
- Jason Gardner, principal, East Mooresville Intermediate School
- Ingrid Medlock, director of human resources
- Mike Royal, principal, Mooresville High School

Impact

Carrie Tulbert, principal of Mooresville Middle School, focused her doctoral work on the impact of digital conversion on collegial relations, an experience that helped her build a strong faculty culture in her school, despite initial resistance to change. Mark Cottone, principal of Park View Elementary School, studied the impact of digital conversion at the elementary level and has led his school to dramatic growth, developing a powerful culture where students thrive academically and love school.

Debbie Marsh has led South Elementary to record-setting student achievement results, and Chuck LaRusso is leading Rocky River Elementary to great success. The principals of both our intermediate schools and the high school, along with other MGSD leaders, are enrolled in the new doctoral cohort, and we feel the impact of their scholarly pursuits as they improve teaching and learning every day.

When we included the goals of our digital conversion—especially student achievement—in the formal curriculum of both graduate programs, we created more opportunities for reflection and added a new power source to drive our work forward. Several of our staff members have served as adjunct professors in the cohorts, which has also added value to our daily work and given them another opportunity to grow.

A team of leaders who are also a team of learners has a huge impact. Every school has shown an upward trajectory in academic achievement. When peers and friends take the leadership journey together, the benefits multiply because of the collaborative synergy between people. And when districts honor the importance of adult learning by investing resources, they send a strong message of caring and support that leads to increased loyalty, pride, and conviction. The result is more energy for improving teaching and learning.

LEADERSHIP VOICE

Learning about Teamwork

By **Robin McElhannon**
Assistant Principal, Corriher-Lipe Middle School, Rowan County School District, and Former Fifth-Grade Chair, Mooresville Intermediate School

Obtaining my master's degree in educational leadership along with ten other MGSD professionals proved to be the best experience of my career. I learned in the master's program and in my work at MGSD that it is impossible for one person working alone to achieve high results. Teaming with a group of like-minded people and sharing a common vision are essential in fulfilling a mission to the highest standards.

The Wingate University program was challenging, but it was taught by some of the most talented educational leaders in our region. It wasn't exactly trial by fire, but I definitely felt singed at times, and my cohort members motivated me to push through when exhaustion set in.

I believe that everyone in my cohort would agree that our MGSD leaders taught us the most practical approaches to leadership.

Imagine having your district superintendent teach you principalship! Dr. Edwards shared his firsthand experiences and instilled values of leadership that helped us to grow, work together, and become better educators.

He even hand-selected books for each of us to read and base our presentations on. It was clear there would be no slacking because he knew each book like the back of his hand! I believe that Dr. Edwards was modeling what good leaders should do—know and respect each person's individuality. He demonstrated how important it is for leaders to understand individual as well as team dynamics.

Since completing the program, I have served on numerous committees and teams and presented at many workshops and conferences, such as the North Carolina Legislators' Retreat.

Return on Leadership Investment: Original MGSD Wingate University Doctoral Cohort

- Dr. Misty Basham was promoted to assistant principal in our sister school district, the Iredell-Statesville School System.

- Dr. Chuck LaRusso was promoted from special education director to assistant principal to principal at Rocky River Elementary School.

- Dr. Debbie Marsh was principal of South Elementary School and has led this school to become a North Carolina Honor School of Excellence.

- Dr. Luke Smith married and relocated to Virginia, where he accepted a promotion as assistant principal.

- Dr. Steve Mauney was promoted from operations director to executive director of secondary education.

- Dr. Todd Wirt, principal of Mooresville High School, was named North Carolina High School Principal of the Year in 2010 and later promoted to assistant superintendent of Wake County Public School System, Raleigh, North Carolina.

- Dr. Carrie Tulbert was promoted from assistant principal to principal of Mooresville Middle School and was named the North Carolina Principal of the Year in 2014.

- Dr. Mark Cottone was promoted from assistant principal to principal of Park View Elementary School and has led this school to become a North Carolina Honor School of Excellence.
- Dr. Alison Schleede accepted a promotion to technology instructional coordinator, Wake County Public School System, Raleigh, North Carolina.

Leadership Academy for Assistant Principals

In many school districts, assistant principals move up the ladder without the benefit of any focused leadership training. At MGSD, we pay direct attention to the development of assistant principals and other evolving district leaders. (See Appendix A for a sample leadership academy agenda.)

Structure

In the MGSD leadership academy for assistant principals, we conduct quarterly training and information sharing sessions and include assistant principals and assistant directors from all levels.

We focus on both horizontal alignment within a grade level or course and vertical alignment from one grade to the next and within a course sequence. For example, when Mooresville students were earning As in Spanish in middle school but then struggling in Spanish in high school, we sat down and mapped out a new vertical alignment. The issue went away.

All our central office leaders participate in the leadership development of their colleagues. The MGSD executive directors of instruction, Crystal Hill and Stephen Mauney, along with the director of human resources, Ingrid Medlock, are responsible for designing the program, and they call on executive team members, principals, and others to lead the sessions.

Impact

It has been exciting to see the growth of MGSD assistant principals as they have stepped up to their leadership roles, influenced by the leadership academy and the leadership synergy in the district and in their schools.

Julie Blocker, the assistant director and career development coordinator at N. F. Woods Advanced Technology and Arts Center, a role very similar to that of assistant principal, provided outstanding leadership for the Career Bridge

Advisory for students and many other aspects of her students' success. Lenoa Smith, new assistant principal at Park View Elementary, showed that she was a quick study, catching on quickly to the MGSD culture. Her leadership is felt every day at Park View and throughout the district. She is a leader who influences a wide circle of colleagues.

Teacher Leader Academy

Since 2008, MGSD has conducted a formal teacher leader program for teams from every school, also led by our executive directors for elementary and secondary education and human resources. The teacher leader program is tightly linked to the work of each school. The goal is to align the growth of our staff with our focus on every child, every day, balanced by the innovation of our digital conversion. (See Appendix B for a sample agenda.)

MGSD recognizes and benefits from the essential leadership role of teachers. Roland Barth has made the point in *Improving Schools from Within: Teachers, Parents, and Principals Can Make the Difference* that principals cannot run schools on their own because schools are far too complex. This is a view we share, and our principals and schools benefit greatly from the contributions and leadership of teachers.

Structure

MGSD principals identify between five and ten teachers from their schools to participate in the teacher leader academy. They select individuals who hold leadership positions or demonstrate leadership potential—people with a positive attitude who are willing to learn how they can impact the cultural environment of their school and district. Initially our teacher leadership programs focused on grade-level and department chairs, but now we are expanding the program to other teacher leaders.

The members of the academy meet three times a year to discuss issues such as what leadership means, what leadership looks like in their schools, and how to develop leadership capacity in different individuals. We choose a book or a variety of articles for discussion, simulations, and direct training.

We discuss the moral imperative in education as well as the importance of building relationships in a caring and loving environment, using the Socratic discussion format along with school team breakout groups. Action plans are implemented at each school, along with training on how to hold peers accountable to best practices in a caring environment and how to use data to drive decision making.

Impact

The MGSD teacher leader academy has had a huge impact. It allows us to identify changes and new directions needed in grade-level and department leadership, while helping teachers learn how to blend data with a tenacious commitment to every student, changing student trajectories and leading them to success. Our 2013 graduation rates of 93.4 percent overall, second in the state, and 97.8 percent for African-American students were direct results of our culture of committed teacher leaders.

Although the vision for change and the initial expectations for change came from our district-level leaders, the transformation took place at the teacher level in the classrooms. Over the years, dozens of teacher leaders have emerged, and they are now actively leading their peers at the school level.

LEADERSHIP IN ACTION

Teacher Leadership in Action

According to Steven Mauney, MGSD executive director of secondary schools:

"Positive peer pressure has been an important outcome of the teacher leader academy, promoting effective classroom instruction and a work environment conducive to student achievement and teacher professional growth. The academy has also helped teachers feel more appreciated and given them a greater voice."

Jody Cohen, Mooresville Intermediate School sixth-grade math chair and the 2014 MGSD Teacher of the Year, has described the impact of the academy as follows:

"Over the years, I have seen the impact of the teacher leader program evolve. We have gained the skills to work in a team environment, and we have gotten better at being leaders.

I have never been hesitant to say what was on my mind, but now I think about what I am saying, knowing that I speak as a leader and not just as a participant. We teachers have grown by interacting with leaders from other schools and from the central office. They treat us as leaders, they talk to us as leaders, and most importantly, they listen to us as leaders."

Annual Conferences

For the past several years, we have run two summer conferences—one for our own staff and one for visitors—that provide multiple opportunities for shared leadership growth in our district.

Summer Institute

The annual MGSD Summer Institute is a three-day, voluntary professional development program for our teachers on digital conversion, with sessions led by teacher leaders and designed around differentiated needs, according to content area, grade level, and technology skills.

Attendees were initially compensated at $50 per day, and after a couple of years, we increased the rate to $100 per day. The number of attendees grew from 225 in 2008 to more than 300 in 2012, representing over 90 percent of teachers. We are now channeling our training to the Common Core Standards and will soon incorporate our new teacher effectiveness criteria.

Because we are constantly evolving, we always need to develop new skills, and the pedagogy of digital conversion means that learning must be ongoing. In addition, new teachers need professional development and emotional support, and new content requires a curricular design that integrates it into our instructional program.

In the early years of digital conversion, the Summer Institute focused on technical adaptation, and then we moved on to content and data. Now our primary focus is on collaboration, inquiry-based active learning, and personalized learning. (See Appendix C for a sample agenda.)

Summer Connection Conference

The MGSD annual Summer Connection Conference is a three-day professional development event for districts from around the country interested in digital conversion. In 2010, we had 250 participants, and this number grew to over 400 in 2013 and 2014, with requests exceeding capacity.

Our teachers and administrators develop and staff the institute, which has profoundly influenced their growth. They lead sessions on a wide variety of topics, from Common Core Standards implementation to new state assessments and digital innovation. (See Appendix D for a sample agenda.)

VISITOR FEEDBACK *"When I was the superintendent of Moore County Schools in North Carolina, I participated in the MGSD Summer Connection conference along with my principals and other staff and visited the district with my school board and others. My goal was to build leadership in my own staff by observing leadership in action at MGSD.*

We came away with the understanding that the conversations at MGSD among teachers and leaders are unlike conversations in other districts. It is clear that leadership is a mutual responsibility granted less by title and more by opportunity. Teachers speak in positive ways about children and are open and honest both about the challenges students are having in the classroom and about the challenges they themselves are having as teachers.

They accept responsibility for students and student learning. They present and discuss their data with remarkable specificity, and they are able to anticipate and answer questions about student performance and expected improvement. They suggest and implement their own solutions to the challenges they identify.

District and school administrators also accept leadership responsibility. They are specific and clear but also empowering. They engage in the dialogue and ask questions, but they listen and affirm the leadership decisions teachers are making. Teachers are part of the conversation, and there is a clear sense that leadership is a team effort. As a result, everyone clearly believes that the students will overcome any challenges.

At one point, we saw Dr. Edwards talking to a teacher about data that showed continued achievement gaps in one subject area, and he said, 'I know you are reflecting on this with me. I'm encouraged, and I have confidence that we will do what we need to do because you are the right leader for this job.'"

—**Dr. Aaron Spence**
Superintendent, Virginia Beach City Public Schools, Virginia, and
Former Superintendent, Moore County Schools, North Carolina

Student and Parent Leadership Development

MGSD offers students a variety of opportunities to participate in leadership development activities. High school students have distinguished themselves by leading student organizations and other initiatives. Middle school students

A gifted and talented student from Mooresville Intermediate School on a weekly visit to a first-grade class at Rocky River Elementary School

participate in a program called The Leader in Me, designed by their teachers, which teaches team building, leadership skills, and leadership awareness in a collaborative environment.

In our intermediate schools, student ambassadors partner with new students to help with the transition and the digital conversion, and they also visit elementary students on a regular basis to provide extra help.

Our parent and teacher advisory committees offer opportunities for dialogue and work that have translated into strong leadership skills for many participants. Parents have formed a Facebook group to stay abreast of school-related issues and mobilize to support funding needs, capital projects, and other issues that require community leadership. Two parents, Lisa Gill and David Coble, who also serves as a Mooresville Town Commissioner, mobilized hundreds of parents to support a bond referendum on the ballot in November 2014, and Lisa leads and edits an MGSD social media group that now has well over 1,000 members.

Our productivity has increased thanks to the many passionate and committed leaders in our teaching and support staff and in our community. To achieve these results, we believe that leadership development must be a formal goal and an informal goal, to highlight its importance and to achieve the best results.

LEADERSHIP VOICE

The Leader in Me

By **Elizabeth Carrigan**
Ninth-Grade Student, Mooresville High School

When I was in middle school, I got to participate in a program called The Leader in Me, which helped me and my peers grow as leaders and develop a new sense of initiative and drive. We learned how to become more active as leaders both at school and in our community, now and in the future.

We are engaged in our world as we learn, and we can connect with other learners across the country and the world. For example, I kept a blog when I was in Japan for six weeks in the summer of 2012, staying connected with my friends back home in the U.S. and sharing information about Japan with them.

Organizational nurturance is an important part of leadership development at MGSD. I monitored the progress of Steve Mauney, MGSD executive director of secondary schools, on his doctoral program to make sure he completed his dissertation.

Steve and his wife adopted two children from China after he started the program, and he coaches basketball on recreational teams, so I knew he needed and deserved a little extra nurturance. It would have been easy for Steve to postpone his goals or drop out of the program, but our supportive culture kept him going through the challenges. Sticking with leaders as they grow is a key indicator of the institutional character of a school system and the level of commitment to leadership development.

Steve is a leader who has grown immensely in the past several years, and I am very proud of him. When we recognized the accomplishment of Dr. Mauney at a school board meeting a full two years after some of his colleagues, the cheers were louder than for any previous graduates. We knew that his leadership journey had been longer and harder, but we felt a shared sense of honor for him and with him.

REFLECTIVE QUESTIONS

1. What external programs are available to your staff to build their leadership capacity?

2. How can you partner with local colleges and universities on leadership development?

3. What programs of leadership development do you offer internally?

4. How do you develop leadership capacity in assistant principals to prepare them for the role of principal?

5. How do you support staff involved in graduate programs?

REFERENCES

Barth, Roland S. (1990). *Improving Schools from Within: Teachers, Parents, and Principals Can Make the Difference.* San Francisco, CA: Jossey-Bass.

Chapter 7

Leading with Formative Power

"The formative power of our leaders connects their learning and the learning of others to our goals and vision every day."

When Carrie Tulbert, the principal of Mooresville Middle School, was planning to be out on maternity leave, we knew we could call on a fine leader, assistant principal Angelo DelliSanti, to take over. Angelo had always been involved in the leadership needs of his school. He had learned from Carrie and others how to be connected to daily school activity at multiple levels and how to use formative data to guide decisions, and he fully embraced the concept that every day offers a new opportunity to learn.

At the same time, expectations were high all around because Mooresville Middle School is a large and complex school, and Carrie was a highly accomplished leader. But Angelo jumped at the formative opportunity. He sought out advice from many people, but he acted like a principal from day one. He was highly visible and accessible, on the sidewalk, in the cafeteria, in classrooms, and in hallways. He constantly interacted with students, teachers, parents, and staff, engaging them in a dialogue about the life and work of his school. He demonstrated calm urgency by focusing his questions and comments on the work of the moment, bringing encouragement with expectations to bear on each situation. And he was always smart enough to say, "I don't know, but I'll check and get back to you." And he did.

None of us knows when we will be called to leadership, but when we are, we must be ready to be leaders. Angelo rose to the occasion with flying colors. In July 2014, he went on to become the principal of Carson High School in neighboring Rowan County, where superintendent Lynn Moody is implementing a digital conversion modeled after MGSD. We were sad to see Angelo go, but we were also very proud of him.

When schools lead with formative power, they use the strength of relevance, the precision of now, and the value of each day's new information to align their work with student and school needs. They constantly fine-tune the effort, with daily calibration of data and human activity to create conditions where learning thrives for students, staff, and leaders.

Formative power links everyone to the leadership model. We at MGSD depend on our vision of shared leadership to take advantage of the talent and energy of our entire workforce.

A Formative Data Engine

As discussed in *Every Child, Every Day*, at MGSD we use formative teaching and learning data to develop a new type of awareness and an ongoing call to action. Adapting our pedagogy with formative data brings precision to our teaching and learning, with information about every student, teacher, content area, class, grade level, and team powering our efforts every day and indicating precisely how everyone is doing.

Our classroom culture is now replete with real-time information that everyone, including students, can use to their advantage. We do not use assumption and intuition to guide our teaching. Instead, we use data that provides a high level of accuracy and efficiency.

Developing a formative data model is not easy, and we still have a long way to go. But the input of many leaders—as opposed to one or two directing the effort from above—has propelled us in the right direction, and we have moved away from the old model of infrequent data analysis toward personalizing instruction every day, based on data. As Hess and Saxberg wrote in *Breakthrough Leadership in the Digital Age*:

> "The air is full of high-flying talk about data driven decision making. The truth is that much valuable data often fall short of helping to inform the learning process even if they serve to evaluate institutions. After all, the once a year model of assessment severely limits how much we can learn about what might have helped certain students master a particular set of skills or knowledge. It makes it tough for schools or systems to adapt in a timely or agile manner.
>
> There are vast new opportunities to revamp what it means to collect and leverage data. After all, ventures like Amazon and Facebook are

not collecting data from their millions of users once a year; they are collecting data every minute, using what they learn to constantly tweak their models, algorithms, and offerings. But such a mindset requires wholly new habits of data collection and use."

A Broad Data Team

Although our principals, assistant principals, department chairs, and grade-level chairs formally lead the development of effective analytics and the timely utilization of information, we also tap into the leadership of MGSD teachers all the time to help refine our formative engine.

We rotate teachers on and off the leadership team to broaden the group at every grade level. Whenever the opportunity arises, we include new teachers and teachers who have a special understanding of certain content or pedagogy. Teachers use a team formative review process, leading each other as they discuss the learning work of students and share data. More and more teachers have been recognized as leaders in this effort, and we have increasingly benefitted from having many eyes on the work and hearts connected for students.

Because we have a huge amount of data available, we need the insight and direction of many leaders to use the information effectively and turn it into a power source for all stakeholders. When different leaders help develop the methodology for managing the flow and allocating resources effectively, the impact is powerful.

LEADERSHIP VOICE

The Leadership Ripple Effect

By **Jody Cohen**
Sixth-Grade Chair, Mooresville Intermediate School

Although I was excited to receive a brand-new laptop at the start of our digital conversion, I was wary about leaving my comfort zone and making so many changes. But the years have flown by, and my former methods of planning and teaching are now obsolete. I have more materials at my fingertips than ever before, and I use formative data to find or create lessons to help each student at his or her level and track progress. As a result, I am a better teacher, student, and colleague.

Before our digital conversion, collaboration among colleagues was almost nonexistent. We planned on our own, mostly using textbooks. We shared test results, but with no real professional connection. Once the digital conversion started, however, we knew we had to work together to be effective and find quality resources to match the curriculum. These tasks were too daunting to do alone.

I'm not sure why, but I soon took to the new ways of thinking and doing. I was not the first to catch on, and I was often frustrated with the changes, joking about needing a 504 for accommodations in the digital world. But at the same time I was willing to try whatever we were given, and there was excitement in the air. With the encouragement of my administrators at the school level and in our central office, I took on a leadership role.

I was leading my grade level and encouraging teachers throughout our school to persevere. I wanted everyone to be excited about the challenges, so I purposefully created a nonthreatening environment in our grade level, encouraging all colleagues to contribute to our weekly meetings and reducing the level of self-imposed intimidation.

Each of us honed new skills, and we grew and succeeded at our own rates, learning together. Some colleagues moved on to different grade levels, where they in turn took on leadership roles, and our school became stronger because of the ripple effect and the constant emergence of new leaders. When I look back, I am amazed at all we have accomplished.

Student Self-Direction

Because MGSD teachers know what students know and don't know, they can adjust the tempo around differentiated learning needs. They know what to teach and whom to teach, and they do not waste time re-teaching those who do not need it. They can zero in and add support efficiently and effectively.

This ability also allows them to authorize students to observe and adjust their own learning—whether that means moving on to another objective or following up on a particular point. Students monitor their learning by closely tracking their data. In our summer Mooresville & Mebane reading program for elementary students, even the youngest learners can pull up their data on their iPads and see their progress and their trajectories. "I'm so proud of them. They know where they are and where they are going," South Elementary assistant principal Cheryl Dortch reported to me.

Almost all our content engines provide formative online assessments that give students real-time personalized data, a formative power that students use at all grade levels and that is also available to parents. The formative power extends to every student, class, and home.

LEADERSHIP IN ACTION

Student Self-Direction in Action

I recently observed several of our teacher leaders using data to teach math more efficiently and effectively. At Mooresville Intermediate School, I watched sixth-grade math lead teacher Jody Cohen work on review with a group of students in preparation for a quiz the next day. The rest of the class was already working on the next objective and would start to review it the following day.

Jody's students have developed the maturity to monitor their own learning, based on data, ask for help when needed, and self-direct. They can keep up with what they know, and they understand when to move on or review.

On another occasion, I observed third-grade co-chairs Carol Elliott and Jennifer Williams at Rocky River Elementary moving ahead quickly with students on one section of the new math standards, knowing that they would need more time for content coming up in the next quarter.

A group of students in this class told me they were getting ready for a math test, and I asked them if they felt ready. They nodded, and one young man added, "We've been taking little quizzes on each objective, and we are over 90 percent on all the objectives." "So, you think you'll do well?" I asked. "We know we will because we're in charge," he replied.

Carol and Jennifer have provided leadership to the entire team, balancing, supporting, and pushing each other while bringing a tighter focus in our weekly meetings on our common formative assessments. They have helped us move from static pacing guides to dynamic pacing and differentiation by student, class, course, or group.

Third-grade co-chair Carol Elliott, working with a student at Rocky River Elementary School

Formative Direction

Formative power applies to the development of leaders at MGSD. As Fullan and Langworthy write in *A Rich Seam: How New Pedagogies Find Deep Learning*:

> "We need new measures not only of students' deep learning outcomes, but also of pedagogical capacity and culture and system capacity. These measures would include the evolving roles of teachers and leaders, the cultural elements described (above), the state of educators' professional learning, and the overall capacities, resources and alignment of the system (region or province, state and/or country)."

Our principals and grade-level and department chairs bolster instruction in particular content areas or courses using formative support for teachers or classes as needed. Formative direction based on differentiated needs is powerful, but it also requires sophisticated analytics and a widespread cultural disposition toward self-improvement.

The formative power of our leaders connects their learning and the learning of others to our goals and vision every day. Our work is driven by the evolving needs of students and schools, and it changes every day. Despite their fixed to-do lists, our teacher leaders take great pride in their flexibility, as they respond to daily needs and proactively make adjustments to improve the working environment and academic outcomes.

VISITOR FEEDBACK *"Organizations and schools that loosen the control and directive atmosphere reap creative, innovative, collaborative, and communicative benefits. MGSD epitomizes an atmosphere of allowing and encouraging leadership from all quarters. That distributed leadership climate has resulted in a school system achieving at all levels."*

—Dr. Alan Lee
Superintendent, Baldwin County Public Schools, Alabama

LEADERSHIP IN ACTION

Formative Direction in Action

At a recent school board meeting, we met a new substitute reporter from our local paper, *The Mooresville Tribune*, for the first time. I welcomed her and introduced myself and the group. We have an excellent relationship with the paper, but over the years, I have learned to be attentive to the dynamics when a reporter is present.

However, in the course of the meeting, some staff members made comments that were less than appropriate in front of a new person we did not know, so in our executive meeting the next day, I offered some formative direction. I encouraged our leaders to look ahead to the time when they might become superintendents themselves, and I stressed that staff need to understand the importance of showing due caution in public meetings attended by reporters they do not know.

Formative Design and Recalibration

It is widely accepted that the value of reflection is underestimated, but at MGSD we have embraced the concept of phenomenological inquiry, the study of consciousness and self-awareness, which leads us to constantly reflect together and recalibrate our instructional design and culture.

Abundant leadership drives our formative instructional design process, a culture mechanism that channels thousands of inputs and connections to create formative power. The process allows us to constantly modify our design for teaching and learning, to harness the insights of every person every day and grow our leadership capacity.

A huge part of our design work is to develop teachers—and, very importantly, students—who utilize their daily learning to lead from within and from all around. Just as kindergartners hold hands and stick together when instructed by their teachers, we stick together, and our many hands raise up the work.

Students working together at East Mooresville Intermediate School

LEADERSHIP VOICE

Recalibrating Support for Special Needs Students

By **Kelly Hildebran**
Special Education Chair, Mooresville Middle School

In the past, we always used to set up staff support for inclusion classes in exactly the same way. The feeling was, "This is how we've always done it, and that's that." But during the digital conversion, we recognized that we needed to step back and allocate time and human resources differently, based on what the data showed us and what students needed.

It has taken time, but we have become used to the idea that we must constantly adjust and fine-tune our work based on data. We know it is the right thing to do. And we have worked to develop a flexible staffing model for our inclusion classes, where team teaching maximizes support for students as their needs change.

Schools often recalibrate instruction annually or quarterly. But at MGSD, we have moved toward situational adjustment on a more frequent—daily and weekly—basis, based on formative data. It took us five or six years, but now we have hit our stride, using formative power to drive instructional practice, pacing, and focus.

We still have further to go, and we strive to support the leadership work of recalibration with the equally important work of formative nurturing. Whether we are dealing with analytics or collaboration, teachers and students always need formative affirmation and direct nurturing from other leaders.

When I was chatting with Dee Gibbs, the principal of N. F. Woods Advanced Technology and Arts Center, a student came up to us and told Mr. Gibbs that Ms. Justice had helped him get caught up. Mr. Gibbs asked if he had also apologized for being rude to her and the boy said that he had and that he had thanked her for staying after school to help him. After the student left, Mr. Gibbs said to me, "This boy has tried everyone's patience, but we know he has a rough home life and no support. We will miss him, but we most definitely want him to graduate. Sometimes we just have to love them across the finish line." I knew I had just witnessed a great example of formative direction in action.

Formative Instructional Design in Action

Every month for the past seven years, we have set aside half a day for professional growth—a learning opportunity that has developed and grown through the influence of our teacher leaders, school leaders, and district leaders.

These leaders collaboratively determine what we need at any given moment with the information we have at hand, planning, implementing, and evaluating professional development activities to meet team and individual needs. As they link learning to the formative development of every stakeholder, they create a vibrant, real-time learning culture for adults and students.

The ongoing conversation about what we need to do to continue to grow has also led to our Summer Institutes and Summer Connection Conferences, in which countless leaders have been involved, providing multiple opportunities for professional growth. As Fullan and Langworthy write in in *A Rich Seam: How New Pedagogies Find Deep Learning*:

> "New measures alone, however, will not change systems. New measures must be combined with real changes in the design and practice of teaching. The quality and nature of professional learning among teachers and leaders is an essential element for effective implementation."

REFLECTIVE QUESTIONS

1. How do you use formative data in your organization?

2. What are you doing to develop leaders who can lead a formative data model?

3. How can you help your students use data to monitor their own learning?

4. What do you do to encourage formative instructional design?

5. How do you ensure that instructional design is adjusted on an ongoing basis?

REFERENCES

Edwards, Mark. (2014). *Every Child, Every Day.* Upper Saddle River, NJ: Pearson Education.

Fullan, Michael, & Langworthy, Maria. (2014). *A Rich Seam: How New Pedagogies Find Deep Learning.* Boston, MA: Pearson. www.newpedagogies.org

Hess, Frederick, & Saxberg, Bror V. H. (2014). *Breakthrough Leadership in the Digital Age: Using Learning Science to Reboot Schooling.* Thousand Oaks, CA: Corwin.

Chapter 8

Tough Stuff

"Tough decisions made in a team environment, focused on what's best for students, usually work."

When I was the superintendent in Henrico County, Virginia, I had to let go a young principal whom I had recruited to work in a very challenging environment. I told him I was proud of his effort and confident that his next position would be a better fit for him at that stage of his development. We both cried. But we stayed in touch. He called me later to catch up, we shared updates on our families, and we continue to maintain respect for each other and a sense of common spirit.

Since the first days of our digital conversion at MGSD, we have dedicated time, energy, and resources to the development of our staff. We knew from the start that it would take longer for some to get on board and that sustained support and patience would be essential. But in our third year, it was time to insist, together, that everyone join the work of growing and changing.

Part of the work of leadership is managing tough calls in an appropriate and respectful manner, to maintain quality as well as care and consideration. It is challenging to promote accountability, responsibility, and transparency, and the effort needs to be supported by defining principles that are clearly understood. At MGSD, those principles are meeting the academic and social needs of every child, every day and supporting each other, even when the messages we have to deliver are difficult.

Leaders must also make tough decisions in other areas besides teacher and staff performance. They have to navigate internal and external politics. They must handle financial problems with skill and manage turmoil around new standards and testing in an effort to ensure the best outcomes for their students.

Teacher Performance

Clear expectations supported by a nurturing culture are the simple but powerful foundation of our culture at MGSD. In our classrooms, standards for student achievement and teacher effectiveness are held in the highest regard by all. But respect for teacher and student work does not mean that leaders look away from areas of need. The willingness to make tough decisions is a leadership requirement, and tough decisions made in a team environment, focused on what's best for students, usually work.

Over the years, we have had to place several teachers on improvement plans, and many have responded to the challenge and elevated their effort and productivity. Our principals have been proud to see them grow as a result of tough and directive feedback. However, some staff members were not able to make the contribution we were looking for, often because they could not adapt to the new focus on effectiveness and productivity, and we had to dismiss them or counsel them out.

Leader Accountability

MGSD has worked diligently to develop the talent and capacity of staff. But our leaders recognize the need to take action when necessary and let someone go when needed. And they understand that extra effort to handle these situations with dignity, respect, and grace should always be part of the separation process.

Separation is sometimes necessary in order to maintain an essential foundation of trust with other staff members and with the community, as well as to stand up for the students. Our leaders have learned to handle these difficult situations appropriately.

Avoiding "Silos"

In many schools and districts, employees organize themselves by department, school, or grade level and stay in their groups with little interaction or communication. Often relationships are strained, and territories are protected. At

Tough Decisions in Action

Teacher A was a fourth-year lateral-entry teacher who loved her subject and worked diligently to give solid lessons. Each year, her test scores were outstanding, but her treatment of students was not in accord with our mission. We sent her to our specialized training, called Capturing Kids' Hearts, and she was excited about the concepts, but they did not come naturally to her. She struggled with classroom management and interactions with parents. Her administrator continued to meet with her to discuss action plans for improvement and guidance. However, although she was high performing, her attitude toward students did not change, so her contract was not renewed. She left teaching completely after this decision was made.

Teacher B was a 12th-year teacher hired late in the school year following the resignation of another teacher who moved to another state. He was the third teacher in the classroom for that school year and had left a tenured position in a neighboring school district in pursuit of a technology-driven culture. He was a very gifted thinker, and his lessons were beautifully crafted to challenge students. But he struggled with some of our average and below-average students, and his classroom management skills were weak. His heart was in the right place, and he genuinely cared about students, but he was not sure how to demonstrate his caring attitude in his classroom management and student interactions. After many meetings and a lack of progress, his contract was not renewed.

Teacher C was a new lateral-entry teacher who had previously worked in many fields outside education and had decided she wanted to teach after working as a substitute. She was all heart and wanted to help students in every possible way. She visited students' homes and tried to support parents. But her lesson planning lacked substance, and her classroom management was inconsistent. Her students loved her, but for the wrong reasons. She met with her administrator multiple times to review a documented action plan, but she did not meet the expectations or complete the action steps, and her contract was not renewed.

MGSD, silos are unacceptable. We promote collaboration across groups, and our teams work to resolve differences, putting the needs of students first and steering clear of the negative silo mentality. But it is important to note that we have had to work hard to achieve this level of cooperation.

Several years ago, the teachers and administrators at Mooresville High School and N. F. Woods Advanced Technology and Arts Center, two faculties that serve the same students, hardly communicated with each other. Although there is still work to be done, we have vastly improved this situation to the benefit of students, with both principals modeling teamwork for all to see.

Similarly, a few years ago, East Mooresville Middle School and Mooresville Intermediate School were far apart and lacked any kind of teamwork, although they are sister schools. Now, thanks to new principals, new grade-level chairs, and a new executive director of elementary instruction, the walls of this silo have come tumbling down. These two schools still have some friendly competition, but they work together on curriculum planning and data analysis and applaud each other at every data meeting.

LEADERSHIP IN ACTION

Leader Accountability in Action

In Mike Royal's first year as the principal of Mooresville High School, he had to non-renew a couple of teachers, probably the hardest thing that he had to do that year. According to Mike, "If we have ineffective teachers, we first provide support to help them grow and improve. Our support system includes mentors and buddy teachers, an ongoing orientation program, an instructional technology facilitator, and a collaborative environment to assist all teachers, especially new teachers. But if teachers do not respond and improve, then it is in the best interest of the students that they leave."

Jason Gardner, the principal East Mooresville Intermediate School, has faced similar situations. "I learned a long time ago one of the basic rules of teacher retention," says Jason. "If you would not want your own child in that classroom, then that teacher should not be in your school. Some administrators might shy away from these tough decisions in an effort to avoid conflict, but at MGSD, we never choose what is easy over what is best for the kids."

Collaboration across Departments

By **Scott Smith**
Chief Technology Officer, MGSD

The digital conversion has brought every MGSD employee to a new level of understanding and appreciation for doing what is in the best interest of every child. Dr. Edwards expects and trusts leaders to excel in their respective areas of responsibility and at the same time cross areas of xpertise.

As the CTO, I oversee all things technical, but I also have responsibility in the areas of media and instructional technology. I have close working relationships with the curriculum and instruction directors, and we collaborate in these areas. These relationships have torn down the walls between departments and allowed all of us to be focused and headed in the same direction.

The focus on meeting the needs of each child has invigorated me to provide the absolute best I can for everyone—no matter if it is fast connectivity, great technical support, or awesome digital resources. In all decisions, we discuss what is best for students, not what is best for the department or the technology. This is a paradigm shift, and it has built a new level of cooperation among team members. It is also a new way of leading for me.

Politics

Within a school district, the internal politics of change are not always straightforward, so it is essential to maintain transparency and openness to ideas coming from different stakeholders. In a major transformative initiative, when leaders are asking staff to do something that is new and difficult, they can expect some pushback and even blowback. Ongoing communication and continual work on shared commitment are essential.

When we first started our digital conversion at MGSD, many teachers and community leaders were uneasy about the changes they would be expected to

School Board Leadership in Action

When I first met Leon Pridgen several years ago, he was not happy with the schools in Mooresville. As an officer of the Mooresville branch of the NAACP, he told me about the concerns of African-American families regarding racial bias, bigotry, achievement gaps, disproportionate suspensions, and poor communication.

We worked together to build better communication processes and improve the situation, with Leon serving in leadership roles on our parent advisory committee and the Mooresville Education Foundation. He was elected to the MGSD school board in November 2013 and is an active and thoughtful leader in our district.

make. So we prioritized clear communication with our school board, parent advisory committee, and other elected leaders. Because we constantly listened and communicated, we were able to get through the politics and the challenges of early implementation.

Leaders must be able to understand and navigate all the local, state, and national political activity that impacts education. Partnerships with chambers of commerce, foundations, and other community groups outside the district not only benefit students but can also help leaders navigate rough political waters.

School leaders generally need to find common ground and build collaborative networks with elected leaders at every level. The well-being of our children, schools, and communities depends on it. If the ultimate goal is to find shared resolutions, leaders must resist the temptation to take a hard line or voice disdain in order to avoid exacerbating difficult situations. In North Carolina, recent legislative changes have made many dedicated educators want to throw up their hands in despair, but as leaders, we have to stay at the table and work with the officials to forge a way forward.

Working hard at compromise and keeping the focus on students is usually a winning strategy, although it is not always easy. For example, when I was the superintendent in Henrico County, I battled with a commissioner over redistricting when I would have been far better off searching for common ground and extending some grace.

MGSD school board member Leon Pridgen and his wife Gail at the school board swearing-in ceremony, December 2013

Conflicts

Conflict is a natural part of any organization, and learning how to handle and respond to conflict is an important part of leadership. When dealing with conflict, I have learned over the years to stay on the high ground, remain respectful and courteous, and demonstrate empathy.

I believe that leaders can successfully resolve conflicts by working with all parties to find common ground for as long as needed. Or they can allow the parties to agree to disagree, while still demonstrating respect and even

East Mooresville Intermediate School principal Jason Gardner and Mooresville Middle School assistant principal Hollis Baker, working together at a principal team meeting

appreciation for each other. I have also learned that ignoring conflict often results in a snowball effect, so conflicts must be dealt with in a timely manner.

Several years ago, when two MGSD teachers could not agree over the direction of their department as it grappled with the challenges of digital conversion and new accountability measures, we tried repeatedly to mediate or move on, but with little success. In the end, we moved one of the teachers to a different school. This decision was not well received, but we had to take action. Both teachers have since done well and are happier and more productive. Sometimes there is no clear path to resolving conflict, but failing to address such a situation only adds to the problem.

Budget Cuts

Four years ago, we lost ten percent of our funding from North Carolina state and local allocations. Other schools across the country faced the same situation. We had to make some very tough decisions, and we let go about ten percent of our full-time staff over the next two years.

Conflict Resolution in Action

A few years ago, the district and I butted heads with one of our town council members, primarily about the partnership between MGSD and the Mooresville Recreation Department and Programs. Later, when the council member was appointed as a North Carolina state senator to finish out the term of a senator who had passed away, we met with him to discuss the impact of state education policy and funding on MGSD and other districts.

We made a sincere effort to provide information and recommendations in line with the interests of our community. He in turn made a sincere effort to identify the information channels he would need in his new assignment. We developed a positive, productive collaboration, moving past our former disagreements, because both parties were committed to successful conflict resolution.

Some cuts were based on performance deficiencies, but in other cases, we had to let go staff members who were doing a good job but had been recently hired. We worked hard to be transparent about the dilemma and communicate that we deeply regretted the hurt and shock involved. However, the tears and pain were excruciating for all involved.

I recall sitting in on a meeting with a principal when she informed a young first-year teacher that she no longer had a job. The teacher began to sob, and the principal and I both tried to comfort her. I told her that we would hire her back if and when we could, and a year later, we were able to hire her back at a different school, where she was recognized as the Teacher of the Year in 2014. Difficult situations like this are part of school life, and learning to work through them, as best we can, is essential for school leaders.

The impact of the budget cuts continues to be tough as of this writing. Our teachers have received no raises for five years, and class sizes are up significantly in grades 4 through 12. More and more employees are struggling to make ends meet, and the situation is wearing on many families. In addition, in our teacher evaluations, we are now required to implement more stringent requirements on the use of student achievement data. Especially during this time of no raises and budget cuts, destructive comments about public education have been hurtful to us all.

In the face of these challenges, it would be easy to allow morale to be damaged and give way to despair, but our teachers and staff have been able to find ways to maintain their momentum and synergy. Our district has received much positive feedback, and our spirits have been lifted by our parents and community, who repeatedly acknowledge our work. When people hear "thank you" often, it makes a difference. We have many reasons to stick together as we work through the tough stuff, and we do.

LEADERSHIP VOICE

Teamwork Between Instruction and Business Departments

By **Terry Haas**
Chief Financial Officer, MGSD

Early in my career as a chief financial officer, I learned that the more I knew about instructional goals, the better able I would be to stretch limited funds. When instruction and business form a team, the students win every time. I have followed this philosophy in every district where I have worked, including MGSD.

This practice served me well during the 2009–2010 school year, which proved to be the most challenging in my twenty-plus-year career. The economy had dropped, and we were faced with drastic reductions from local and state funding sources. All 115 districts in North Carolina were dealing with similar reductions. We expected push-back from our families and community as we discussed the difficult choices that had to be made to keep our budget balanced—choices that involved cutting people or technology.

Conversations began at the executive staff level and moved to the full leadership team. We determined that major staffing reductions would be needed to balance the budget. Although we were growing in size, we would not be able to add custodial, maintenance, or technology staff, and we had to cut teachers and teacher assistants. Cutting staff is never easy, but in previous years, we had laid the groundwork by keeping staff and the community informed and providing a transparent financial process, which greatly eased the difficult situation.

> When the discussion moved to our parent advisory group, Dr. Edwards and I expected that some parents would want to eliminate our digital program and maintain our staff ratios, but the group was united in requesting that we maintain the digital program. Although the parents did not like the staff reductions, they supported our decision to increase class sizes to deal with the budgetary shortfall.
>
> As difficult as these decisions were, they were the easiest part of the process. The hardest part came when we had to call in excellent and hardworking staff to inform them they were being cut. This was particularly tough because ours is a small town where people bump into each other all the time. But I believe we all did our best to continue providing a quality learning experience to every child under very challenging circumstances.

Testing and Standards

The testing load on MGSD and other schools has increased greatly over the years, with more and longer tests. In North Carolina, we are now required to administer end-of-course and end-of-grade tests for all students in grades 3 through 12, and more tests were added recently, with a host of North Carolina final exams in content areas we had not previously been testing.

In addition, we are managing new standards and a standards landscape that is constantly changing. A year ago, North Carolina was a Common Core Standards state, with the governor and other leaders fully committed to the new standards. Then came a major political push-back from conservative elected officials, and an action late in the session by the North Carolina General Assembly directed the state board of education to pull back. So the legislative message was confusing, to say the least.

Because we have been gearing up for two years for the Common Core Standards, the confusion has created many problems. But we have taken the stance that whether we follow new North Carolina Standards or Common Core Standards, we know that our students will benefit from a more rigorous and application-based curriculum. Meanwhile, we make every effort to communicate to our teachers what is going on and to support their growth and learning.

We work hard at keeping our teachers informed and enlisting their leadership to handle the pressure and create the best conditions for our students, despite the difficult circumstances. We take heart by holding hands and sticking together, a strategy that works for us in many situations.

When I interviewed Carrie Tulbert for the position of principal at Mooresville Middle School, I asked her if she would be able to help every teacher in the building become a better educator. She immediately said yes, as if no other possibility existed. But when I mentioned certain teachers who had mediocre reputations, she gradually realized that I was talking about a significant part of her responsibility as a principal.

Carrie came to recognize that teachers who are "good enough" in some environments may not be the very best we can offer our students. This understanding led her to several tough decisions, but they were also some of the best decisions she has made for our students.

REFLECTIVE QUESTIONS

1. How you do you manage tough decisions regarding teacher performance?

2. What is your approach to conflict management in your organization?

3. Does your staff consciously work to avoid the "silo" mentality?

4. What strategies help you manage internal and external politics?

5. How have you used teamwork to help address budget cuts?

Chapter 9

Second-Order Leaders

"Second-order leaders must be fluid and dynamic. They must learn and evolve as they lead."

In November 2012, a small team of MGSD leaders flew to Washington, D.C., to conduct a panel discussion on digital conversion at the annual Jeb Bush Education Summit.

I was accompanied by Carrie Tulbert, principal of Mooresville Middle School; Samone Graham, biology teacher at Mooresville High School; Troy Eckles, president of the Mooresville High School student body; and Mark Miller, an eighth grader at Mooresville Middle School. We were all a little nervous, since the gathering included Secretary of Education Arne Duncan, several governors, and many national education leaders.

We answered questions about our leadership journey and the transformation of our district. Troy started out slow, with some understandable jitters, but after a few questions, his leadership instincts and aptitude kicked in. When the moderator asked the last question, about why the digital conversion was so important, Troy quickly said to the rest of the panel, "I've got this one."

Troy told the audience, "My family didn't have what some other families have, but my school, my teachers, and my district gave me something that every kid needs, a level playing field. And I'm taking full advantage of it, just like kids all over this country will if they have the chance."

New Leaders for New Learning

The work of MGSD teachers, students, and staff has changed dramatically since we began our digital conversion. This transformation has required us to embrace "second-order change" and "second-order leadership," which require flexibility, creativity, and new thinking. The importance of second-order change in today's schools has been emphasized by many researchers, including J.T. Fouts and the National Academy for Academic Leadership.

First-order leadership, focused on a linear, hierarchical, and repetitive work environment, did not align with the new learning dynamic in our schools or give students the range of opportunities they needed for success.

In the new student work environment, with its opportunities for creativity, collaboration, and research, leaders must lead learning, create individual and collaborative projects, and develop an environment where shared leadership is embraced throughout the organization. Many school reform efforts have fallen short because of inattention to second-order change management issues such as these.

LEADERSHIP VOICE

Teaching Teachers

By **Dakota Smith**
Senior, Mooresville High School

During the first semester of 2014, when I was working on the help desk at my school, I volunteered to help teachers who struggled with some of our software. I set up a schedule during second block, with Keynote on Mondays, iMovie on Tuesdays, Numbers on Wednesdays, Pages on Thursdays, and GarageBand on Fridays. I asked teachers who were interested to set up an appointment for me to visit their classrooms and help them with the apps. I don't drive, so I could only provide assistance to teachers on our Main and Magnolia campuses.

This was important to me because as a school of excellence, we have been granted the use of technology, and we should take full advantage. There are endless ways to teach students with the applications that we hold within these laptops, so every teacher should know exactly what the technology is capable of doing.

It has taken MGSD years to build a second-order change culture to lift up innovation, productivity, and student achievement, but today our leaders work together to build the new culture and structure. With our focus on second-order leadership, greater expertise has developed throughout our faculty, students, and staff. As Thomas and Brown suggest in *A New Culture of Learning*, a digital environment can provide new, interconnected organizational structures in which expertise is widely dispersed:

> "In nearly every aspect of digital culture, structures are emerging that provide concerted cultivation for both general attitudes about learning and specific approaches to skills or areas of interest. Unlike in past decades, however, concerted cultivation in the twenty-first century will value peer-to-peer interaction and the fluid nature of collaboration."

Our distributed and formative second-order leadership culture is at the heart of the improved student performance we have seen in our district, as shown in our student's performance on the North Carolina state tests in the 2013–2014 school year.

MGSD End-of-Grade Improvements, Third Grade, 2013–2014

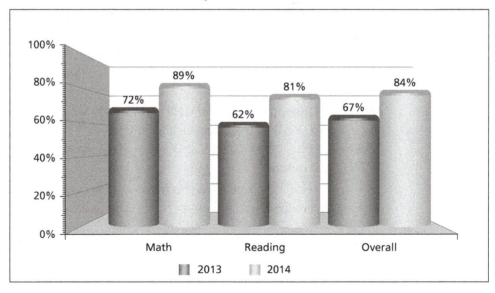

MGSD End-of-Grade Improvements, Grades 4–6, 2013–2014

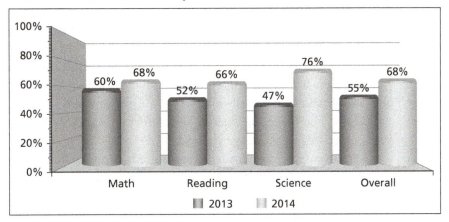

MGSD End-of-Grade Improvements, Grades 7–8, 2013–2014

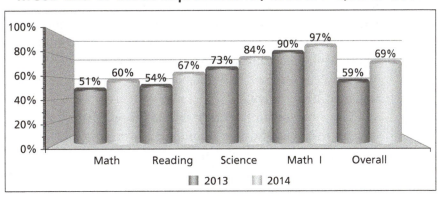

MGSD End-of-Grade Improvements, Grades 9–12, 2013–2014

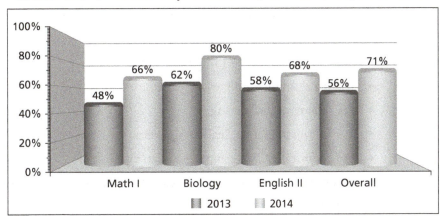

Fluid Leading and Learning

In a fluid and dynamic school culture, second-order leaders must be energetic and motivated. They must learn and evolve as they lead. Leadership is no longer static, and leaders must be able to embrace ambiguity. Just as leaders expect students and teachers to learn though inquiry and investigation, they themselves have to be comfortable with not always having the answers and with working to clarify solutions. They have to develop the comfort level and the skills to investigate, adapt, and integrate change successfully.

For example, when leaders are unsure how a new digital resource works, they must be confident and determined that they will figure it out, and they must have a flexible working disposition that allows them to call on students or colleagues to help troubleshoot as needed while everyone gets up to speed.

This may sound easy, but it is not. Getting used to not having all the answers and shifting gears when things go wrong are big adjustments for many educators, and the situation calls for ongoing training, planning, and leadership.

In addition, second-order leaders must be able to guide collaborative student groups while simultaneously facilitating a productive workflow. They must juggle resources, engagement, and collaboration while ensuring individual and collective academic achievement.

The ability of our leaders to lead in this way has modeled for teachers and students that constantly reexamining our work and making adjustments are integral parts of everyone's daily task.

Characteristics of Second-Order Leaders

- Have high aspirations
- Believe in a philosophy of directional nurturance
- Are comfortable with ongoing change
- Are constantly reexamining the work
- See fun as an integral part of learning
- Are nurturing and caring
- Are willing to assume leadership roles
- Are comfortable with sharing leadership
- Recognize that it is everyone's responsibility to lead and to develop leaders
- Take an across-the-board team approach

The author and Mooresville High School graduate Troy Eckles, discussing the Mooresville & Mebane Summer Literacy Lift program at South Elementary School

Our leaders constantly consider and reconsider how best to handle change, using fluid and nimble strategies, clarifying expectations, and building support. As Hess and Saxberg wrote in *Breakthrough Leadership in the Digital Age*:

> "As learning science and technology advance, new possibilities will keep emerging, creating new opportunities to support great teaching and learning. Leaders who possess an understanding of learning science and who have cultivated the ability to diagnose and rethink learning problems will be equipped to leverage new tools, seek smarter solutions, and transform schooling to improve learning."

Teacher Leaders

Teaching students how to collaborate and also work independently requires a second-order leadership approach. MGSD teachers design our classrooms for collaboration by pushing desks together or using tables. They develop activities that include both independent work and fluid collaboration, aligned to content objectives with formative data.

Our teacher leaders have had to learn on the run, surrounded by change, constantly reframing their views about pedagogy and tools in light of our every child, every day vision while at the same time pursuing the highest standards. They have become part of an organic team, sharing with colleagues the focus on pushing the work forward.

Teachers who lead collaboration among their colleagues have become central to our instructional program. Because our classes are infused with formative information, we rely on teacher leaders to sort and analyze data for and with each other. This is not a sporadic or occasional activity but constant and urgent work.

Teacher leaders map out curriculum, plan and deliver internal and external professional development, help select staff and administrators, and lead the development of an evolving pedagogy that depends on pervasive leadership.

LEADERSHIP VOICE

Always Learning

By **Steve Stith**
Social Studies Department Chair,
Mooresville High School

My district's digital conversion began at Mooresville High School, where I have taught for the better part of 25 years. Faculty at the high school were issued laptops during the 2007–2008 school year, and during that first year, professional development activities were devoted to understanding the computer's applications and possible uses in the classroom. It was an exciting time to be teaching but also one wrought with fear and uncertainty.

The digital conversion was going to be a game-changer in ways few could foresee at the time. But because it was in the best interest of our children, I embraced the challenge. Today I am still analyzing my practice and continually learning from experience, and I am proud to be involved with a school system that emphasizes a process of continuous improvement.

> Recently, my efforts were validated when my principal invited me to be part of a five-teacher team that traveled to Missouri over the summer to train an entire high school staff in digital implementation. I welcomed the opportunity to collaborate on a national level with other professionals while further examining my own practice.

Media Specialists

In our open media center model, students stream in and out of our media centers all day long, and our media specialists have taken their game to a whole new level. No longer just the keepers of the books, they have expanded their capacity as second-order instructional leaders, embracing our digital conversion, facilitating individual and collaborative student research, and participating in professional learning communities to integrate their work with that of teachers and students.

They are also involved in a national effort called Project Connect, sponsored by Follett and the American School Library Association and designed to redefine the role of libraries and media specialists, which brings together superintendents and media specialists from around the country. In workshops and on panels, our media specialists have described their new role at MGSD and how they have evolved as leaders, modeling an individual and collective disposition of service and flexibility. At a recent *School Library Journal* Leadership Summit, a panel of five MGSD media specialists and CTO Scott Smith described their work as a second-order change model for the future.

Principals and Assistant Principals

MGSD principals know that developing a second-order leadership culture takes constant attention, and they understand that the journey is a long and winding road. They are always learning on the job, designing and redesigning professional development that addresses differentiated needs, recognizing that some grade levels and departments may need more direction and support than others.

They also learn to get out of the way when necessary, a skill that relies on detailed knowledge of their schools. And in every conversation—about budgets, hiring, or pedagogy—they talk about every child.

They contribute to second-order change by being truly invested as learners, using directional nurturance, believing in the value of collaborative leadership,

Leading and Learning in Action

In June 2013, I met with Crystal Hill, our executive director of elementary education, and Chuck LaRusso, principal of Rocky River Elementary, to discuss the drop in end-of-grade results at Rocky River. We were all surprised by these results because Rocky River had previously been either at the top of our elementary schools or neck-and-neck with the leading school. I spoke to Chuck about the need to pull his leadership team together and build out a detailed plan for improvement, while assuring him of my ongoing support.

Chuck responded by taking full responsibility and agreeing that the results were unacceptable. I told him I had no doubt that he and his team would rise to the occasion with the support of Crystal, who was also accountable. Crystal mentioned that she and Chuck had already started work on a new action plan.

All test scores in North Carolina had dropped 35–40 points after the Common Core Standard Assessments were introduced, but although our composite scores ranked third in the state, we were eager to improve. Rocky River has the highest poverty level of any MGSD school, with over 28 percent of students receiving free and reduced lunch. However, the previous year more than 92 percent of students had passed math and reading.

In October 2013, when I visited Mrs. Campbell's classroom at Rocky River, I saw her and the specialists tutoring small groups of students. She told me that the specialists had set aside part of their planning time each day to help in the classroom and that students were making great progress in reading. "We knew we needed to add an extra boost to support the third-grade team, and everyone jumped in," she said. As we left the classroom, Chuck acknowledged how proud he was of the specialists for contributing the extra time.

When I visited the school in March 2014, Chuck introduced me to a parent tutor he had recruited to support the third-grade team and to provide one-on-one support. He explained that when he and his team developed the action plan, they decided to ask their PTA to identify some volunteers who could give a few hours a week. "We offered some training and figured out a schedule, and it's working well," he said.

By June 2014, Rocky River had seen a substantial jump in scores, as a result of much dedication and second-order leadership.

Rocky River Elementary Third-Grade Improvements, 2012–2014

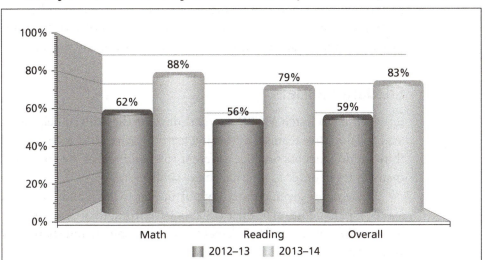

and working at leadership development. For example, a few years ago, when two teacher leaders at the high school level moved into instructional technology facilitator positions, their former principals and assistant principals had to search for and develop new teacher leaders. This was one of their most important second-order leadership responsibilities.

District Leaders

MGSD's entire central office team has grown exponentially in their embrace of second-order leadership. Other districts are constantly recruiting them away—three assistant principals have become principals or directors in other districts over the past two years—which motivates us to discover and develop new leadership talent as well as work hard to retain the leaders we have.

Because we are all growing together, we are passionate about the shared work of developing new leaders. Our directors and executive directors, along with our chief technology officer, chief financial officer, and public information officer, work as a team to provide services and directional nurturance to each principal and to many teams within each school.

Our central office staff have to be active listeners and highly engaged at multiple levels with each school and department. Our instructional program is based on their constant collaboration to make sure we are all aligned with the needs of our schools and community. Coordinating the work of hundreds of leaders has helped our central office staff develop outstanding collaborative skills while maintaining a laser focus on academic achievement, as we share the work and the fun.

Student Leaders

It is exciting to watch MGSD students develop the skills to help each other and lead collaborative teams, but this is a learning curve that takes time. So, starting in third grade, students practice different roles and repeat the collaboration process many times in order to internalize the skills.

Students are given constant opportunities to learn and provide second-order leadership. In addition to their collaborative work, they demonstrate leadership in the way they speak, conduct research, master content, and share their knowledge with others.

When the president of the United States visited Mooresville Middle School in June 2013, he spent most of his time talking to students. Students described the work they were doing, showed President Obama how they connect math concepts to real-world problems, and demonstrated how they use online content, analytics, and middle school culture to advance learning. Teachers did very little talking. It was inspirational to hear students articulate what they were doing and why it was important.

Just before the president spoke in the gymnasium, a special education student from Mooresville Middle School stepped up to the microphone and led the Pledge of Allegiance. Although she hit a couple of small bumps, she electrified everyone with her outstanding leadership skills.

LEADERSHIP VOICE

Thank You for the Leadership Opportunities

By **Troy Eckles**
Mooresville High School Graduate and Howard University Sophomore

Coming from an underprivileged home, I struggled because I did not have the resources other students had, such as a home computer and money for tutors. But at MGSD, I had teachers who wanted to see me succeed, and I had access to technology. Many students like me felt that they had a chance to better themselves with these resources.

I have always felt that I needed to prove myself at home, at school, and in my community. I wanted to be the best in the class, and I also got involved in a lot of extracurricular activities. But I didn't want to be just another person in a club. I wanted to lead the club. I took on a lot of roles as the president, which was not easy. Often I felt overwhelmed, but I continued on, knowing that one day my hard work would be noticed and pay off.

I was very surprised when I was asked to fly to Washington, D.C., to speak about our digital conversion. That was big. Someone was relying on me to represent MGSD positively in our nation's capital. It was my chance to prove that I could be of some use. And as president of the student body, I was asked to speak in front of my class in preparation for our graduation. It was then that I realized this was real. People believed in me. As I stood before my class, it hit me that the easy part was coming to an end, and I was there to lead them to the finish.

After graduation, I thought that MGSD might have forgotten about or replaced me, but I was mistaken. I received an email asking if I wanted a job teaching in an elementary literacy mentoring program over the summer. They said I would be a great mentor for these children, and I fell in love with the job. Making an impact on young children's lives really had an effect on me, but I learned more from them than they learned from me. Later that summer, I received another email, asking me to speak on a panel about the digital conversion. It was an honor to give my point of view.

MGSD has given me countless opportunities to show that I have something to offer and has told me that I can do anything. I have come so far. The best part about my journey is knowing that I am not the only one. MGSD creates new leaders just like me every year.

I have always considered myself to be a leader because I set high goals for myself, and I am very persistent. But I have learned that leadership involves much more than titles. Being a leader means setting an example for others to follow, taking on responsibilities, and maintaining a positive image in the community.

Hundreds of MGSD students participate in a wide variety of co-curricular activities, and the growth of student leadership has brought additional value to a wealth of opportunities. More than 400 students participate in the band, choral, and drama programs at Mooresville High School, more than 200 belong to the MGSD Junior Naval ROTC, and several hundred embrace leadership roles in student athletics. Our coaches and directors consistently focus on building student leadership.

As Fullan and Langworthy wrote in *A Rich Seam: How New Pedagogies Find Deep Learning*:

> "Learning to learn, where students become meta-cognitive observers of their own and others' learning processes, is a fundamental goal in the new pedagogies. The goal is not only to master content knowledge; it is to master the learning process.
>
> Learning to learn requires that students begin to define their own learning goals and success criteria; monitor their own learning; critically examine their own work; incorporate feedback from peers, teachers, parents, or simply other people in general; and use all of this to deepen their awareness of how they function in the learning process. As students make progress in mastering the learning process, the teacher's role shifts gradually away from explicit structuring of learning tasks, and towards providing feedback, activating next-level learning challenges, and continuously developing the learning environment."

Support Staff Leaders

At MGSD, we encourage and rely on leadership among our support staff to move us toward second-order change. We recognize their efforts at luncheons and award ceremonies throughout the year because we know that we could not move the ship forward without them.

Support staff leaders attend to hundreds of important details every day, facilitating the efforts of students and instructional staff to pursue academic excellence. They are essential team players in the work of education, and they know it.

Replication of Second-Order Change

Although MGSD is a relatively small district, with 6,000 students, dozens of districts large and small, urban and rural, are building out their own digital

Lee Hill, custodian supervisor, and Teddy Culbertson, maintenance/construction/ hardware specialist, at the June 2013 operations department appreciation luncheon

conversions based on our model—from Poplar Bluff, Missouri, with 5,200 students; to Moore County, North Carolina, with 12,500 students; to Vancouver, Washington, with 22,700 students; to Baldwin County, Alabama, with 30,000 students; to Baltimore County, Maryland, with 109,000 students. In addition, many districts throughout the Canadian province of Alberta are working with the MGSD model.

Leaders from these districts have participated in our Summer Connection Conference and have gone on to create their own versions of digital conversion, often working in partnership with MGSD leaders.

We are often asked whether large districts can use our model successfully. The district that has really doubled down on replication is the sixth-largest school district in the United States, with 206,000 students—not exactly a mirror image of MGSD. Houston Independent School District (HISD) has launched one of the most ambitious digital conversion initiatives ever undertaken.

HISD veteran superintendent Dr. Terry Grier has visited MGSD several times, along with school board members, principals, teacher leaders, and district and community leaders, and they have developed a plan to replicate the MGSD model. This is a huge task, but results so far are promising, and new leaders are evolving.

HISD Powers Up

By **Dr. Terry Grier**
Superintendent, Houston Independent School District

We launched our HISD PowerUp initiative in the summer of 2013, with educators from 11 high schools participating in a pilot one-to-one computing program designed to provide anytime/anywhere learning to 18,000 students. In the summer of 2014, as of this writing, we are preparing to bring on another 21 campuses, and by the 2015–2016 school year, we expect that all 44 HISD high schools will be on board. We have faced many challenges and reaped many rewards as we have introduced 21st-century learning into our schools.

Finding the Funding

The first challenge we faced was money. When I joined the district in 2009, I found that computer technology was a low priority and antiquated, and we had gone without E-Rate funding for 12 years. With 80 percent of our students qualifying for free and reduced lunch, most children had limited or no access to computers at home and no Internet connectivity.

Shortly after I arrived, we recovered our E-Rate funding, and in 2012, voters passed a $1.9 billion bond issue that included a $100 million technology infrastructure upgrade. We boosted our district broadband capacity, made sure each campus had effective wireless service, and created a one-to-one laptop initiative along with free or reduced-price Internet connectivity for families at home.

Moving to a Uniform System

HISD is one of the most decentralized districts in the United States, and site-based management meant that the district had installed a hodgepodge of infrastructure, hardware, and software over the years. Although most students had never owned a laptop, one campus with parents of means wanted students to be able to use their own laptops instead of devices purchased by the district.

But we knew that a uniform system was essential, so we worked hard to convince school board members that we were not trying to re-centralize the system and take decision-making authority away from principals.

Campuses were equipped with district-connected infrastructure, and all students were required to use the same district-purchased and district-programmed HP laptops. Teachers were trained by DiscoveryEd and by an outstanding team from the Mooresville Graded School District. Software was evaluated and approved at the district level, and schools were required to fund technical and instructional specialists to deal swiftly with their individual needs—a huge shift from how the district had conducted business in the past.

Managing the Paradigm Shift

As the paradigm changed, we had to manage expectations carefully and ask some key questions. How do we change the culture to solicit buy-in from principals and teachers? How do we successfully bring on board students and families who have limited technology experience? How do we make sure our focus on curriculum and instructional resources match and maximize the new technologies?

A core group of early adopters eagerly embraced the new vision, many late adopters were not fully on board, and some resisters pushed back—with principals, deans, and assistant principals falling into each category. This range of responses plus the teacher turnover inherent in any school system—in our case, 10 to 20 percent annually—meant that training, professional development, and communication were key.

We developed a strong training program that incorporated a team of second-order leaders who were responsive to the unique needs of each staff member and each campus. For our initial five-day intensive training with DiscoveryEd, we formed a PowerUp Leader Corps for each of our 44 high schools with one teacher from each core subject—language arts, math, science, and social studies—who created model classrooms to serve as teaching laboratories.

The model classrooms vividly illustrated the strength and potential of PowerUp through the first phase of the program, with 44 strong second-order leaders making the difference between success and failure during our first-year rollout.

Our communications department devised a sweeping internal and external information program with a comprehensive website (houstonisd.org/PowerUp). Parents and students were given mandatory instruction in digital etiquette, the digital footprint, and social media responsibility, and were required to sign contracts of understanding.

We like to say that PowerUp is about more than the devices. So we communicated to students, families, and teachers that the software and the devices work together with skillful teachers to personalize learning, create richer and more relevant lessons, and link learning to life.

HISD has made great progress and is leading the way for large districts moving to a digital conversion model. Dr. Grier describes the current status as follows:

"Our digital conversion has been hard and challenging work. But our progress toward transforming our classrooms, the new collaboration among our educators, and the deep connection of our students to a whole new world of learning have been inspiring and motivating.

One of our greatest sources of pride has been in creating second-order leadership, which has manifested itself in sometimes unexpected and heartwarming ways. At our Young Women's College Preparatory Academy, the students have become the teachers. In this role-reversal, the girls show teachers how to use their favorite websites and software, demonstrating collaboration in a way we never imagined. Those breakthroughs are making PowerUp an extraordinary experience in HISD.

The digital transformation of any school system is essential for 21st-century learning, to prepare students for higher education, the workplace, and our shrinking world. But the shift is not easy, even for small districts, and the longer you wait, the more difficult it becomes.

The challenges we faced in Houston will present themselves on a different scale in every district and will require courage, creativity, and never-ending commitment, because digital learning is a lot like parenting. You can never stop doing it, even when your children seem ready to make it on their own or are competent adults."

REFLECTIVE QUESTIONS

1. How can your organization move toward second-order leadership?

2. What can you do to help your leaders lead and learn at the same time?

3. How can you help your staff become comfortable with a fluid and dynamic culture?

4. What challenges would you anticipate in replicating the MGSD model?

5. How will the size of your district impact your journey toward digital conversion?

REFERENCES

Fouts, J. T. (2003). *A Decade of Reform: A Summary of Research Findings on Classroom, School, and District Effectiveness in Washington State.* Seattle, WA: Washington School Research Center at Seattle Pacific University.

Fullan, Michael, & Langworthy, Maria. (2014). *A Rich Seam: How New Pedagogies Find Deep Learning.* Boston, MA: Pearson. www.newpedagogies.org

Hess, Frederick, & Saxberg, Bror V. H. (2013). *Breakthrough Leadership in the Digital Age: Using Learning Science to Reboot Schooling.* Thousand Oaks, CA: Corwin.

National Academy for Academic Leadership. *Leadership & Institutional Change,* www.thenationalacademy.org/ready/change.html.

Thomas, Doug, & Brown, John S. (2011). *A New Culture of Learning: Cultivating the Imagination for a World of Constant Change.* Lexington, KY: CreateSpace.

Epilogue

Every fall I look forward to our convocation before school starts, when we bring employees and the community together to celebrate our accomplishments, honor the previous year's teacher of the year and principal of the year, and kick off the year on a high note, supported by our band, chorus, and naval JROTC color guard.

In 2014, two days before this annual event, I decided to notch things up a little. I emailed our leaders that we would be starting off the convocation with a "dance off" or "spirit off" competition, with a dinner as the prize for the winning team, and I gave each group a time slot of about a minute and a half to "do their thing."

We typically start the convocation at 9:00 a.m., but at 8:45 a.m. on the big day, we could already hear the chant "South is in the house, South is in the house" coming from the South Elementary team, waiting outside the auditorium.

At 9:00 sharp, the South Elementary staff came marching in, wearing yellow florescent t-shirts and yellow day-glow bracelets, clapping tambourines and shaking pom-poms and shakers in the air. We scrambled to get the sound board on, and a few minutes later, the bass and soul from "Everyday People" filled the auditorium.

Then the chant "We are N. F. Woods, we are N. F. Woods" blended in with the vibe as the N. F. Woods staff came dancing down the aisles, followed by the staffs of East Mooresville Intermediate School, Mooresville Middle School, and Mooresville High School, streaming in with their tambourines and shakers. The staffs of Park View Elementary and Rocky River Elementary rocked in, led by Park View principal Mark Cottone dressed as a patriot (complete with top hat), followed by language arts teacher Susie Hudson sporting a red Mohawk and dozens of spirit leaders dressed in goofy costumes.

When "Shout" came on over the sound system, the Park View team ran onto the stage and danced like crazy. South Elementary staff, prancing and dancing, rocked it wide open with acrobatics and crazy costumes, and then came the Rocky River team with principal Chuck LaRusso crawling across the stage.

When we heard the Isley Brothers singing the line "A little bit slower now," the teams from Mooresville Intermediate School and East Mooresville

Mooresville Intermediate School teacher Ellecia Sims, South Elementary School teachers Lauren Pollock, Scott Roper, and Kitch Deaton, and Park View Elementary School principal Mark Cottone at the 2014 convocation

Intermediate School sprinted out across the front row and up onto the stage, with East Mooresville teacher Justin James beating out the beat on a portable electronic drum set.

Suddenly the Mooresville Middle School team was up, with teacher Allison Field doing six forward handsprings across the stage as "Footloose" blasted through the speakers. Then the onstage group was joined by staff from all our support programs—transportation, technology, nutrition, maintenance, central office, before and after school, and student services—with everyone giving it their all.

By this time, everyone in the house was up on their feet, rocking and stomping. Then, to the sounds of "Devil with a Blue Dress," N. F. Woods teacher Darren Bridges—6 feet 3 inches tall and 240 pounds—came dancing on stage wearing a blue dress and a blonde wig. The entire Mooresville High School faculty danced in unison across the stage, followed by the MGSD bus drivers grooving to "Rock It Down," with bus driver James Morton taking center stage and bringing the house down.

For the next five minutes, all the teams jammed together on stage, with community leaders, the mayor, the county commissioners, school board members, and local business leaders coming up front and clapping and dancing. It was impossible to pick one team over another, but our local businesses later generously donated the funds to pay for a dinner for all employees.

This was the most fun and spectacular display of shared leadership I have ever seen. Everyone in the auditorium became part of the vibe and was lifted by everyone else. I can still feel the beat, see the smiles, hear the laughter, and remember the joy of being fired up together for our mission of every child, every day.

Assistant Principal (AP) Leadership Academy Agenda

Session 1: Leadership from a Global Perspective, November 12, 2013

Sections	Topics	Length	Time
Purpose of AP Leadership Academy	• Introductions • Review of agenda and objectives • Executive director's leadership charge	10 min.	8:30–8:40
Superintendent's Address	• What makes a great leader? • Reflections on leadership journey	30 min.	8:45–9:15
AP Professional Learning Community on Assigned Articles Socratic Seminar Style	• "Social and Emotional Learning for Leaders" • "The Significance of Leadership Style" • "School Leadership around the World"	45 min.	9:15–10:00
BREAK		10 min.	10:00–10:10
Discussion of *Becoming a Resonant Leader* Pages 1–68	• Leading for real: Becoming the leader you most want to be • Resonant leadership: What it takes • Listening to your wake-up calls: Staying awake, aware, and ready to learn	60 min.	10:10–11:10
Reflection Time	• How are you currently demonstrating resonant leadership?	5 min.	11:10–11:15
Leadership Updates and Announcements	• Proper investigation techniques • School safety and new gun laws	25 min.	11:15–11:40
Questions and Answers	• TrueNorthLogic • Email communications • General issues	15 min.	11:40–11:55
For the Good of the Order	• Debrief and review • Prepare for next session February 27, 2014, "Leading for Change" Discuss pages 69–150 in *Becoming a Resonant Leader*	5 min.	11:55–12:00
Informal Sharing and Fellowship with Colleagues	• Lunch	30 min.	12:00–12:30

REFERENCES

Cherniss, Gary. (April 1998). "Social and Emotional Learning for Leaders," *Educational Leadership*. Alexandria, VA: Association for Supervision and Curriculum Development.

Goldman, Elise. (April 1998). "The Significance of Leadership Style," *Educational Leadership*. Alexandria, VA: Association for Supervision and Curriculum Development.

McKee, Annie, Bovatzis, Richard E., & Johnston, Fran. (2008). *Becoming a Resonant Leader: Develop Your Emotional Intelligence, Renew Your Relationships, Sustain Your Effectiveness*. Boston, MA: Harvard Business School Publishing.

Stewart, Vivien. (April 2013). "School Leadership around the World," *Educational Leadership*. Alexandria, VA: Association for Supervision and Curriculum Development.

Session 2: Leading for Change, February 27, 2014

Sections	Topics	Length	Time
Purpose of Leadership Academy: Review	• Reflections from beginning of the year and last session • Review agenda and objectives	10 min.	8:30–8:40
AP Professional Learning Community on Assigned Reading Scott Smith Stephen Mauney Crystal Hill	• *Change Leader* • "Sharing the Secrets" • "When Leadership Spells Danger"	45 min.	8:45–9:30
Chief Financial Officer's Address Terry Haas	• How can you be a change agent and still be fiscally responsible? • Q&A	30 min.	9:30–10:00
BREAK		15 min.	10:00–10:15
Discussion of *Becoming a Resonant Leader* Pages 69–150	• Seeing your dream: Building an energizing personal vision • Appreciating your real self: Seeing the whole picture • Philosophical orientation questionnaire • You just won the lottery! ☺	60 min.	10:20–11:20
Reflection Time	• How are you currently demonstrating resonant leadership personally and professionally?	10 min.	11:20–11:30
Executive Director "Talk"	• What does it mean to take initiative for professional growth as a school leader and still support the principal?	15 min.	11:30–11:45
Questions and Answers	• TrueNorthLogic • General issues	15 min.	11:45–12:00
Lunch, Informal Sharing, and Fellowship with Colleagues	• Debrief and review • Prepare for next session April 3, 2014, "Becoming a Resonant Leader" Discuss pages 151–213 in *Becoming a Resonant Leader*	30 min.	12:00–12:30

REFERENCES

Fullan, Michael. (2011). *Change Leader: Learning to Do What Matters Most.* San Francisco, CA: Jossey-Bass.

Good, Rebecca. (April 2008). "Sharing the Secrets," *Principal Leadership.* Reston, VA: National Association of Secondary School Principals.

Heifetz, Ronald, & Linsky, Marty. (April 2004). "When Leadership Spells Danger," *Principal Leadership.* Reston, VA: National Association of Secondary School Principals.

McKee, Annie, Bovatzis, Richard E., & Johnston, Fran. (2008). *Becoming a Resonant Leader: Develop Your Emotional Intelligence, Renew Your Relationships, Sustain Your Effectiveness.* Boston, MA: Harvard Business School Publishing.

Session 3: Becoming a Resonant Leader, April 3, 2014

Sections	Topics	Length	Time
Welcome and Reflections	• Reflections from last session, "Leading for Change" • Review of agenda and objectives	10 min.	8:30–8:40
AP Professional Learning Community on Assigned Reading Todd Black Stephen Mauney Crystal Hill	• *The Wounded Leader* • "Making the Most of It" • "The Power of Gentleness"	45 min.	8:45–9:30
Public Information Officer's Address Tanae McLean	• How do we ignite resonance through effective relationships with stakeholders while still being ethically responsible as school leaders? • Q&A	30 min.	9:30–10:00
BREAK		15 min.	10:00–10:15
Discussion of *Becoming a Resonant Leader* Pages 151–213	• Becoming a resonant leader: Taking your desires from awareness into action • Igniting resonance: Creating effectiveness in teams, organizations, and communities	60 min.	10:20–11:20
Reflection Time	• Video • Where will you go from here?	10 min.	11:20–11:30
Executive Director "Talk"	• How will you deliberately demonstrate resonance in your current leadership role?	15 min.	11:30–11:45
Questions and Answers	• Setting PDP goals for next year • Support staff evaluations • General issues	15 min.	11:45–12:00
Lunch, Informal Sharing, and Fellowship with Colleagues	• Thank you for your participation this school year!	30 min.	12:00–12:30

REFERENCES

Ackerman, Richard H., & Maslin-Ostrowski, Pat. (2002). *The Wounded Leader: How Real Leadership Emerges in Times of Crisis*. San Francisco, CA: Jossey-Bass.

Daresh, John C. (January 2001). "Making the Most of It," *Principal Leadership*. Reston, VA: National Association of Secondary School Principals.

Heller, Daniel A. (May 2002). "The Power of Gentleness," *Educational Leadership*. Alexandria, VA: Association for Supervision and Curriculum Development.

McKee, Annie, Bovatzis, Richard E., & Johnston, Fran. (2008). *Becoming a Resonant Leader: Develop Your Emotional Intelligence, Renew Your Relationships, Sustain Your Effectiveness*. Boston, MA: Harvard Business School Publishing.

Teacher Leader Academy Agenda

December 4, 2013
11:30–3:00

Discussion of *The 5 Levels of Leadership: Proven Steps to Maximize Your Potential*

By John C. Maxwell

Level 1: Position (Rights)

- Employees must follow because they have no choice.
- Position is a poor substitute for influence.
- Those in authority are bosses rather than leaders.

Level 2: Permission (Relationships)

- Employees choose to follow.
- This level is not about preserving a leadership position but about getting to know people and figuring out how to get along with them.
- You can like people without leading them, but you cannot lead people well without liking them.

Level 3: Production (Results)

- Employees follow because they respect the accomplishments of leaders.
- Leaders get things done, beyond creating a pleasant working environment.
- This level is a requirement for organizations to move to higher levels of effectiveness.

Level 4: People Development (Reproduction)

- Employees follow because they appreciate the support of leaders.
- Effectiveness is based on empowering others.
- Teamwork is a key characteristic.

Level 5: Pinnacle (Respect)

- Employees follow because they admire their leaders and what they stand for.
- Effort, skill, intentionality, and a high level of talent are required.

- Leaders develop other leaders who in turn develop more leaders (Level 4).
- Leaders often transcend their positions, organizations, and even industries.

Group Self-Assessment

From *The 5 Levels of Leadership*

Levels	Group Responses
1	76%
2	70%
3	67%
4	26%
5	46%

Individual Assessments and Personal Reflections

- Take ten minutes to review your personal response.
- Look at each section of the assessment in terms of levels.
- What is your current level of leadership?
- How does your current level of leadership impact your school's leadership culture?

Group Activity

- Work in school-based teams.
- Review assessment items related to Levels 2–4.
- For each level:
  - Identify the three statements that most closely mirror your school's leadership culture.
  - Identify one or two areas that need improvement.
  - Be prepared to discuss.

Video

Watch the video accompanying *The 5 Levels of Leadership*.

Table Discussion

- Based on the video and your reading of *The 5 Levels of Leadership*, choose a discussion topic from the list below.
- Discuss the topic as it relates to your roles as teacher leaders in your school and in your grade levels, departments, and professional learning communities.
- Create an action plan for your group outlining steps you can take to move your collective leadership toward Level 4.
- After 30 minutes, share your plan and the most significant points of your discussion with the larger group.

Discussion Topic 1

- Maxwell says:
  - If you want a pleasant work environment, achieve Level 2.
  - If you want a productive work environment, achieve Level 3.
  - If you want a growing work environment, achieve Level 4.
- How would you describe the work environment:
  - In your grade level, team, and/or department?
  - In your school?
- What can you do to move toward or maintain a growing environment?

Discussion Topic 2

- Maxwell contrasts what Coach Pat Summit calls "leading by assumption" with "leading by knowing" (e.g., knowing where your people are).
  - Which kind of leading is more effective with your students and why?
  - As teacher leaders, how can you incorporate more "leading by knowing" in your grade, department, PLC, and school?

Discussion Topic 3

- Which factors in your work environment (grade level, department, team, and school) bring out the best in people?
- Which factors are missing?
- What can you do as teacher leaders to foster an environment that brings out the best in people?

Discussion Topic 4

- Maxwell says that effective leaders never lose sight of results as the goal. What do you think of this statement?
- He also says, "What got you here, won't keep you here." What does he mean by this? How does this statement apply to your grade level, department, team, and school?

Questions and Wrap Up

REFERENCE

Maxwell, John C. (2011). *The 5 Levels of Leadership: Proven Steps to Maximize Your Potential.* New York, NY: Center Street.

Summer Institute Agenda

July 28–30, 2014

Presenters

Teacher leaders, media coordinators, instructional technology facilitators, guidance counselors, assistant principals, principals, university professors, independent contractors, service providers, North Carolina Department of Public Instruction staff

Pre-K–Grade 6

DAY 1	DAY 2	DAY 3 (half day)

Preschool

Cool tools: iPad apps Kahoot & Popplet	CSEFEL	Team collaboration
Early learning foundations	CSEFEL	Team collaboration
Project-based learning	CSEFEL	Team collaboration
Project-based learning	CSEFEL	Team collaboration

Grades K–1: Choices

Kindergarten

Oral & written response to text	Building the Write Foundation	Team collaboration
Oral & written response to text	Building the Write Foundation	Team collaboration
Math instructional strategies	Building the Write Foundation	Team collaboration
Cool tools *or* Wixie	Building the Write Foundation	Team collaboration

Grade 1

Cool tools *or* Wixie	Building the Write Foundation	Team collaboration
Drew Polly, UNC Charlotte College of Education	Building the Write Foundation	Team collaboration
Oral & written response to text	Building the Write Foundation	Team collaboration
Oral & written response to text	Building the Write Foundation	Team collaboration

Grades 2–3: Choices

Grade 2

Building the Write Foundation	Drew Polly, UNC Charlotte College of Education	Team collaboration
Building the Write Foundation	Wixie *or* Multimedia tools	Team collaboration
Building the Write Foundation	Student ownership in assessment *or* Multimedia tools	Team collaboration
Building the Write Foundation	Wixie *or* The Daily 5 instructional model	Team collaboration

Grade 3

Building the Write Foundation	Wixie *or* Multimedia tools	Gateway Project (Wixie)
Building the Write Foundation	Drew Polly, UNC Charlotte College of Education	Team collaboration
Building the Write Foundation	Student ownership in assessment *or* Multimedia tools	Team collaboration
Building the Write Foundation	Wixie or *The Daily 5* instructional model	Team collaboration

Grades 4–6: Choices

Grades 4–6 ELA

Building the Write Foundation	Blendspace for lesson delivery, *or* Multimedia tools, *or* Student feedback tools	Team collaboration
Building the Write Foundation	*The Daily 5* instructional model, *or* Using Google sites in the classroom, *or* Instructional strategies in the 1:1 classroom	Team collaboration
Building the Write Foundation	Blendspace for lesson delivery, *or* Multimedia tools, *or* Student feedback tools	Team collaboration
Building the Write Foundation	Student ownership in assessment, *or* Using Google sites in the classroom, *or* Instructional strategies in the 1:1 classroom	Team collaboration

Grades 4–6 Math

TenMarks	Blendspace for lesson delivery, *or* Multimedia tools, *or* Student feedback tools	Team collaboration
TenMarks	Student ownership in assessment, *or* Google sites in the classroom, *or* Instructional strategies in the 1:1 classroom	Team collaboration
Drew Polly, UNC Charlotte College of Education	Blendspace for lesson delivery, *or* Multimedia tools, *or* Student feedback tools	Team collaboration
Drew Polly, UNC Charlotte College of Education	Student ownership in assessment, *or* Using Google sites in the classroom, *or* Instructional strategies in the 1:1 classroom	Team collaboration

Grade 5 Science

Reading for information strategies	Read, Write, and Think Like a Scientist	Team collaboration
Maximizing Discovery Education Techbook™	Read, Write, and Think Like a Scientist	Team collaboration
Maximizing Discovery Education Techbook™	Blendspace for lesson delivery, *or* Multimedia tools, *or* Student feedback tools	Team collaboration
Maximizing Discovery Education Techbook™	Student ownership in assessment, *or* Using Google sites in the classroom, *or* Instructional strategies in the 1:1 classroom	Team collaboration

Grades 7–12

DAY 1	DAY 2	DAY 3
Angel for new employees	Intermediate Google tools: Calendar, Voice, & Drive	Team collaboration
Blendspace for lesson delivery	Instructional strategies in the flipped classroom	Team collaboration
Video tools: eduCannon, EDpuzzle, YouTube	Beginner Google tools: Drive, Calendar, Gmail	Team collaboration
Multimedia tools: Animoto, ThingLink, Mural.ly, Voki	Create & lead staff development for your department or school	Team collaboration
Online discussion and backchannel tools: Today's Meet, Collaborize, edModo, Chatzy, Padlet, RealTimeBoard	25 ways to use Google apps in your classroom	Team collaboration
Presentation tools: Google Presentations, Animoto, Prezi, Capzles, HaikuDeck	Google research strategies	Team collaboration
Student feedback tools: Kahoot, Socrative, Poll Everywhere, Quizlet, VoiceThread, Geddit	Podcasting with iTunes	Team collaboration
Student feedback tools: Kahoot, Socrative, Poll Everywhere, Quizlet, VoiceThread, Geddit	Teaching the outliers: EC, ESL, gifted, inclusion and co-teaching strategies	Team collaboration
Student feedback tools: Kahoot, Socrative, Poll Everywhere, Quizlet, VoiceThread, Geddit	Interpreting student data to improve instruction	Team collaboration
	Applying for professional certifications: Google, Graphite, Discovery, BrainPop, Common Sense, NBCT, etc.	Self-guided

Music

Google basics or Creating video for instructional purposes	Choice	Team collaboration
Working with EC students	Choice	Team collaboration
21st-century music room	Choice	Team collaboration
21st-century music room	Choice	Team collaboration

Art

Google basics or Creating video for instructional purposes	Choice	Team collaboration
Working with EC students	Choice	Team collaboration
MGSD art website	Choice	Team collaboration
MGSD art website	Choice	Team collaboration

Health and PE (HPE)

Google basics or Creating video for instructional purposes	Choice	Team collaboration
Working with EC students	Choice	Team collaboration
HPE instructional best practices	Choice	Team collaboration
HPE instructional best practices	Choice	Team collaboration

Guidance Counselors

Naviance	504	Plan
Naviance	504	Plan
Naviance	Google intermediate	
Naviance	Google intermediate	

REFERENCES

Angel Learning, www.angellearning.com

Animoto, animoto.com

Blendspace, www.blendspace.com

Building the Write Foundation Professional Development Course. Silver Spring, MD: Discovery Education.

Boushey, Gail, & Moser, Joan. (2006*). The Daily 5: Fostering Literacy Independence in the Elementary Grades,* Portland, ME: Stenhouse Publishers.

Capzles, www.capzles.com

ChartGizmo, chartgizmo.com

Chartle, www.chartle.net

Chatzy, www.chatzy.com

Collaborize Classroom, www.collaborizeclassroom.com

CSEFEL (Center on the Social and Emotional Foundations for Early Learning) http://csefel .vanderbilt.edu

EdModo, www.edmodo.com

EDpuzzle, https://edpuzzle.com

educannon, www.educanon.com

Geddit, letsgeddit.com

Haiku Deck, www.haikudeck.com

Infogr.am, https://infogr.am

Kahoot, www.kahoot.com

Maximizing Discovery Education Science Techbook™ for High School, Professional Development Course. Silver Spring, MD: Discovery Education.

Mural.ly, https://mural.ly

Naviance, www.naviance.com

Padlet, padlet.com

Poll Everywhere, www.polleverywhere.com

Popplet, http://popplet.com

Prezi, prezi.com

Quizlet, quizlet.com

Read, Write, and Think Like a Scientist Professional Development Course. *Discovery Education Science Techbook™ for High School.* Silver Spring, MD: Discovery Education.

RealtimeBoard, https://realtimeboard.com

Scoop.it, www.scoop.it

Socrative, www.socrative.com

Symbaloo, www.symbaloo.com

Tagxedo, www.tagxedo.com

TenMarks, www.tenmarks.com

ThingLink, www.thinglink.com

Today'sMeet, https://todaysmeet.com

VoiceThread, voicethread.com

Voki, www.voki.com

Wixie, www.wixie.com/wixie

Summer Connection Conference Agenda

Level 1 Administrators

Second-Order Leadership
- Casting and mobilizing the vision and building community support
- Finding and sustaining a digital environment

District Implementation of a 1:1 Initiative
- Collection and deployment
- Logistics 101
- Parent communication, problem solving, finding the win–win
- Social media issues and digital citizenship

Changing the Teaching and Learning Environment
- Personalized learning
- What does an effective digital classroom look like?

Raising the Bar
- Dealing with the data
- Formative assessments and evaluation

Redefining Roles and Relationships
- Relationships and collaboration
- Repurposing resources
- The 21st-century team

Staff Development
- Designing ongoing district professional development
- Evaluation and accountability
- Key performance indicators and timeframes

Hear from the "Real" Experts

Level 2 Administrators

The Culture Shift
- Dream school
- Collaboration
- Changing the teaching and learning environment

School Implementation of a 1:1 Initiative
- Implementation team
- Repurposing resources
- Logistics
- Staffing and organizing a help desk
- Discipline and responsible use policy

School-Based Leadership
- Casting and mobilizing the vision
- Change leadership
- Building parent and community support
- Building teacher leader capacity

Redefining Roles and Relationships
- Relationships
- Collaboration and the 21st-century team
- School culture development
- An effective digital classroom environment

The Bigger Picture
- Digital citizenship
- Collaboration in a professional learning community
- Using data to drive instruction

Modifying the Instructional Environment
- The 1:1 teaching environment and instructional trends
- Personalized learning and instructional strategies

Staff Development
- Designing meaningful professional development
- Teacher evaluation and accountability
- Key performance indicators and timeframes

Hear from the "Real" Experts

Book Talk for Professional Learning Communities

Chapter 1: Distributed Leadership and High-Performance Teaching and Learning

1. What does the author mean by distributed leadership?
2. How does distributed leadership differ from traditional leadership?
3. How does distributed leadership contribute to high-performance teaching and learning?
4. Why do today's schools need a different view of leadership?

Chapter 2: Leaders with a Shared Vision

1. Which groups can share in the distributed leadership model?
2. How can principals and teachers model leadership?
3. Why is a shared vision of leadership essential?
4. How does distributed leadership impact students?

Chapter 3: Aligning Leaders with the Mission

1. What does the author mean by aligning leaders with the mission?
2. Why is alignment necessary?
3. What are some practical ways educators can align their work with their mission?
4. What is "brilliant consistency" and why is it important?

Chapter 4: Cultural Conditions for Shared Leadership

1. What cultural conditions are needed to support distributed leadership?
2. How does school culture impact the leadership model?
3. To what extent are the cultural conditions described by the author prevalent in schools?
4. What is the relationship between leaders and culture?

Chapter 5: Everyday Paths to Leadership

1. What are some informal ways teachers can develop as leaders?
2. What are some informal ways principals and assistant principals can develop as leaders?
3. How does distributed leadership impact hiring procedures?
4. How does distributed leadership help schools build capacity?

Chapter 6: Formal Programs of Leadership Growth

1. How do formal programs of leadership growth affect school culture?
2. What formal growth pathways can districts make available to teachers and administrators?
3. How can districts support teachers and administrators who are involved in external degree programs?
4. In what ways do internal district conferences help teachers and administrators grow as leaders?

Chapter 7: Leading with Formative Power

1. What does the author mean by formative power?
2. Why is it important to involve many leaders in analyzing student data?
3. Why is constant recalibration necessary to support student achievement?
4. How can students use data to become more independent learners?

Chapter 8: Tough Stuff

1. Why is leader accountability essential in schools?
2. How can leaders help their schools avoid the "silo" mentality?
3. How does teamwork help leaders navigate difficult situations?
4. In what positive ways can leaders approach school politics and conflicts?

Chapter 9: Second-Order Leaders

1. What does the author mean by second-order leaders?
2. Why are fluidity and flexibility needed in second-order leadership?
3. How do the characteristics of second-order leaders influence student performance?
4. How can other districts move toward second-order leadership?